It Happened in Tennessee

It Happened in Tennessee

James Ewing

Rutledge Hill Press
Nashville, Tennessee

Published in Nashville, Tennessee, by Rutledge Hill Press, Inc.,
211 Seventh Avenue North, Nashville, Tennessee 37219

Typography by ProtoType Graphics, Inc., Nashville, Tennessee.

Library of Congress Cataloging-in-Publication Data

It happened in Tennessee.

    Includes index.
    1. Tennessee—History—Miscellanea.   2. Tennessee—
Biography.   I. Ewing, James, 1917–
F436.5.17   1986   976.8   82-22094
ISBN 0-934395-31-4

Manufactured in the United States of America
2 3 4 5 — 98 97 96 95

Introduction

A short time after my book, *A Treasury of Tennessee Tales*, was published it occurred to me that, with Tennessee Homecoming '86 in the offing, and people's thoughts directed to their roots, there was a need for a different kind of book. It would be similar to *Tennessee Tales* to the extent that it would relate true stories that have happened during the long history of our state, but it would be different in that it would use stories that would come from the people themselves.

I conveyed the idea to Lawrence M. Stone, publisher of Rutledge Hill Press, which had published my first book, and he immediately saw the potential of such a book. The question was: How do you go about finding stories of the kind we wanted?

We agreed that the most practical way would be to send out a news release. A release was sent out over Mr. Stone's signature. It explained that we were looking for true happenings from every part of the state. "They do not have to be historically significant but they must be interesting," he wrote.

Something else that captured the interest of potential storytellers was the fact that we were offering $200 in cash awards to those whose stories were considered the best.

The media came through in fine style, and it wasn't long before dozens of submissions were arriving each week at the offices of Rutledge Hill Press. My job was to go through these manuscripts and choose those that I considered to be among the best. To those stories that were sent in, we added six from the *Tennessee Folklore Society Bulletin*. This journal is a rich treasure of interesting stories and historical information.

The selection process was a gargantuan task. There were some stories that were just not particularly interesting. But there were many that were, and we used as many of them as we could. There were quite a number of interesting stories that were not used for one reason or another. First, we wanted a good representation from Middle, East and West Tennessee, and we needed to balance the serious stories with others that were written in a lighter vein. We also needed a balance of long, medium-length and short stories.

I certainly appreciate everyone who sent us a story and I hope the above will explain the fact that if your particular story wasn't used it doesn't mean that it was not a good story.

We had the further task of picking the first, second, third and fourth best stories for the prizes, and that, too, was a difficult job, but it was one in which the publisher also participated.

We adopted a set of criteria for this, including quality of writing, interest, and whether major revisions were needed. After careful consideration, the following awards have been made:

First place: "The Lieutenant Salutes the Flag," submitted by Judith Ann Biddle, Seymour;

Second place: "The First Funeral of Bush Breazeale," submitted by Deloris Jo Stafford, Harriman;

Third place: "Jonesborough Rock," submitted by J. D. Anderson, Elizabethton;

Fourth place: "Christmas at Ozone," by Freelan E. Lewis, Crossville.

In addition to saying "thank you" once more to everyone who submitted a story, I wish to say a special thanks to United States Senior Judge Charles G. Neese of Nashville, Doug Morris of Knoxville, Josephine Neel Wallen of Murfreesboro, and Judith Ann Biddle of Seymour for their multiple submissions that were used.

Credits were given whether the senders wrote the stories in full or in part or simply sent in some facts from which the stories were written. Those with no credit were written by me.

James Ewing

Contributors

Anderson, J. D. "Jonesborough Rock"
Askew, Beverly. "Ghost in the Cemetery"
Badgett, Nan N. "The Wampus Cat"
Barry, William L. "Tennessee's Biggest Man"
Benson, Ruth. "True to Her Yankee Soldier Man"
Biddle, Judith Ann. "For Love of Elsie"
_____ . "The Lieutenant Salutes the Flag"
Broadrick, Estelle. "A Miracle Named Elvis"
Browning, Elizabeth Jones. "Don't Ye Tetch It"
Butler, Ellis O. "The Free State of Scott Rejoins Tennessee"
Conley, Mrs. Victor G. "Great Jumping Bullfrogs!"
Conyers, Helen Stewart. "Git Along, Little Goosie"
Covington, Ruby Nevil. "Tennessee's Sleeping Beauty"
Forrester, Rebel C. "The Night They Moved the Courthouse"
Hearne, Mary Glenn. "Mother Knew Best"
Hoobler, James. "Tennessee's Biggest Man"
Howell, Roger K. "What Mr. Wooten Saw"
Lewis, Freelan E. "Christmas at Ozone"
Lowe, Maggie J. "Who Tore Jim Norvell's Coat?"
Mathes, C. Hodge. "Jeff Howell's Buryin'"
Moore, Kathleen. "Robert Allen, Self-taught Genius"
Morris, Doug. "The Battle of Athens"
_____ . "Millard Fillmore Buchanan"

Table of Contents

CHAPTER 1
Unforgettable Characters: Memorable Tennesseans

Tennessee's Biggest Man

*Thanks to James Hoobler, State Historian,
and William L. Barry, Lexington*

Lexington's Mills Darden wasn't the world's largest man and he wasn't the world's tallest man, but he appears to have been the tallest large man and the largest tall man on record.

The 1986 edition of the *Guinness Book of World Records* lists Darden as having been seven feet, six inches tall, and having weighed 1,020 pounds. John Brower Minnoch, at 1,400 pounds, weighed more, as did three others, but the tallest of that quartet was only six feet, two inches.

The world's tallest man, according to *Guinness*, was Robert Wadlow of Alton, Illinois. He measured eight feet, eleven inches, but weighed a mere 491 pounds at his heaviest.

Laura Waddle of near Lexington, who has done extensive research on Mills Darden, wrote in a brochure that he was born October 29, 1799, near Rich Square in Northampton County, North Carolina. Between 1827 and 1830, he and his first wife, Mary, moved to Tennessee. They had at least three daughters and possibly other children at that time.

The 1830 census showed him as living in Madison County but at some point before 1840 he moved to Henderson County, where he lived the rest of his life, married two more times, and raised several more children.

As a farmer, Mills Darden was a hard worker, requiring

three men to bind grain as he cut it. There were many stories about his great strength. According to one, he single-handedly pulled a loaded wagon from a mud hole, presumably after a team of mules had failed.

There were also stories of his great appetite, some no doubt exaggerated, but Mrs. Waddle said that one article that sounded credible to her reported that his usual breakfast consisted of a dozen eggs, thirty "buttered biscuits," ten slabs of bacon, and two quarts of coffee, along with a gallon of water.

One of the more believable stories about the size of his clothing was that in 1839 a coat made for him was borrowed by three men, each weighing more than 200 pounds, that they buttoned the coat around themselves, and walked around the courthouse square in Lexington.

Darden continued to grow in size well into his forties, and some said his increasing size made it difficult for him to do farm work. About 1845, at the age of forty-six and weighing a reported 870 pounds, he moved to Lexington and opened a tavern and inn.

The 1850 census showed that he owned real estate valued at $500 (roughly equivalent to $25,000 today), that he was the father of seven children, one of them an adult, one an infant, and five of them schoolchildren. The stagecoach business was booming and so he did a thriving business.

About 1853 he moved to the country again, settling on a farm about eight miles southwest of Lexington where he lived until his death in 1857 at the age of fifty-eight.

What was Mills Darden really like? A few clues give an indication. He refused to weigh, at least after he had reached his greatest size, but acquaintances devised a novel way of estimating his weight. They measured the tension of the spring under the seat of his wagon while he was occupying it, pressed the seat down to the same level with stones after he had left it, then weighed the stones. The weight was well over 1,000 pounds.

Being so large was an ordeal for him and he was sensitive about it. To him it was a handicap and he treated it in the same manner that some physically impaired heroes and heroines of today treat theirs. He overcame his handicap by becoming a good citizen, husband, and father, and by going about his everyday life in as normal a way as he possibly could.

A brochure published by the Beech River Watershed Development Authority, Lexington, reported in part:

> Mills Darden would not want to be remembered for his size. That was a burden fate placed upon him—but a burden which he surmounted by determination and strength of will. Farmer, businessman, property owner, educated (he bought many books), for more than a half century Darden lived with his infirmity, which in fact resulted from a glandular deficiency. He earned a livelihood, reared and educated his children and proved decisively that a crippling handicap can be overcome.

According to the brochure, the earliest "extant" newspaper account of his life appeared in the *Lexington Reporter* of August 27, 1875, eighteen years after his death. It quoted a contemporary press account of his burial, saying that the funeral service was preached with the "Masonic fraternity" in attendance and dressed in full regalia. It was also reported that carpenters making his coffin used 156 feet of lumber and it required seventeen men to place his body in it.

Darden was laid to rest January 27, 1857, beside his first wife, and small gravestones were erected. Although the markers were accidentally destroyed in the course of cultivation, through the contributions of the Tennessee American Revolution Bicentennial Commission, Beech River Watershed Development Authority, Central State Bank, and Mrs. W. W. Dunivant, the owner of the site, the graves of Darden and his wife have been carefully restored.

This was done "as a memorial to the effort of one man,

afflicted in body, but not in mind, to live usefully, rear a family, earn a living, and serve his God under burdens of the flesh and of the spirit—and to succeed."

Adolph Ochs and His Castle in the Air

Tennessean Adolph Simon Ochs epitomized in his life the nineteenth-century American go-getter philosophy expressed by Henry David Thoreau in *Walden*:

> If one advances confidently in the direction of his dreams, and endeavors to live the life which he has imagined, he will meet with a success unexpected in common hours. . . . If you have built castles in the air, your work need not be lost; that is where they should be. Now put the foundations under them.

A poor Knoxville boy, born of German-Jewish immigrant parents in Cincinnati in 1858, Ochs started out at age eleven as a part-time newsboy earning twenty-five cents a day from the *Knoxville Chronicle*. But he had a dream, he put the foundation under it, and he became publisher and owner of the prestigious *New York Times*.

After selling newspapers for three years, Ochs marched into the office of the *Knoxville Chronicle's* publisher, Captain William Rule, and said he wanted a full-time newspaper job. Asked by the surprised and bemused publisher what he could do, young Ochs said he could sweep the floor. He was hired—at the same $1.50 a week he had been receiving. But for a boy who had dreams of emulating Horace

Adolph Ochs, publisher of the New York Times, *who began his career at age eleven as a newsboy for the* Knoxville Chronicle.
[United States postage stamp issued September 17, 1976, 158 million minted]

Greeley, the New Hampshire farm boy who had become publisher of the *New York Tribune*, this job offered the opportunity to learn everything there was to know about a newspaper.

A few months later, the publisher, impressed at his eagerness to learn and his willingness to work, promoted Ochs to "printers' devil," a job requiring his doing whatever the printers told him to do, from cleaning the press roller to delivering messages and fetching sandwiches and beer. But it opened a new opportunity for him, the chance to learn the printer's trade, something he did in an amazingly short period of time. Before his sixteenth birthday, "Ochsie," as he was known to his fellow workers, had become a full-fledged printer, moving his foreman to remark jokingly that he feared that Ochs would some day have the foreman's job; but the lad was already thinking of far greener pastures.

He informed publisher Rule that he planned to try for a job with the South's leading newspaper, the *Louisville Courier-Journal*. The publisher regretted the decision and said so in glowing terms in a brief editorial, which, plus a letter from Rule, was all Ochs needed to land the job.

Although he became assistant foreman of the composing room within a month, Ochs ran into a detour in his career. His father, Captain Julius Ochs, a brilliant man in many ways—capable of speaking six languages, for instance— had difficulty providing the necessities of life for himself, his wife, and the five remaining children in Knoxville. Ochsie sent his family his savings of fifty-six dollars. Broke and homesick, he quit his job and returned to Knoxville, just six months after he had left.

Embarrassed by the thought of asking to return to his former paper, he took a job with the *Knoxville Tribune*. There he met Colonel John MacGowan, a gifted editorial writer. Although the colonel was much older than young Ochs, a close friendship developed, leading to an opportunity for Ochs to join the colonel and a third person, Franc

Paul, in buying a newspaper in Chattanooga, the *Dispatch*. The two older men raised the capital and Ochs provided his talent as a printer and his enthusiasm.

In the 1870s Chattanooga was still suffering from the effects of the Civil War. It was difficult for any business to survive during that period, and the *Dispatch* proved no exception. It went bankrupt, but Ochs managed to borrow the use of its presses, which he used to put together a city directory.

In the process of gathering information for the directory, he met many influential business people, including a bank officer at the First National Bank. Hearing that the *Chattanooga Times*, a four-page daily with a circulation of 250, was up for sale, Ochs went to the banker and said he needed $300. The officer demurred, but young Ochs was fast becoming an eloquent salesman, and he finally got the money. That gave him $250.00 to buy the paper; $25.00 to pay a long overdue debt to the Associated Press; $12.50 for legal fees; and $12.50 for operating capital.

He prevailed on his old pal John MacGowan to serve as editor, at $1.50 a day, and a third person to serve as reporter. It was a real struggle. Soon Ochs was paying his employees through a barter system, in which he obtained credit slips from merchants for advertising, the slips being redeemable for groceries and dry goods.

But by putting out a quality newspaper, circulation and advertising grew, as did the prestige of the *Chattanooga Times*. Ochs decided a modern building and press were needed, and so he set out to construct a six-story granite building with a golden dome.

Soon, however, the bright outlook took a dark turn. Ochs became involved in a land deal and was left holding the bag for a $103,000 loan. Although his newspaper was making an impressive $25,000 a year, his debts were growing and he gave serious thought to filing for bankruptcy. Only his pride and his determination prevented it.

Certain he would never get out of debt through his earnings from the *Chattanooga Times,* he had a novel idea: If one good newspaper would not make enough money to pay his debt, maybe two newspapers could. So he began a search for a paper with a growth potential. Never one to shy away from thinking unthinkable thoughts or dreaming impossible dreams, he even considered a New York paper.

In his position as the head of a well-known newspaper in Chattanooga, Ochs had met many influential people. One such person, Harry Alloway, told him that the *New York Times* was for sale, and he put in a good word for Ochs among some of the paper's biggest stockholders. While riding in a parade in Chattanooga, Ochs had met President Grover Cleveland and they became friends. Ochs wrote letters to the president and to fifty other influential people asking for their support in his efforts to convince the *Times'* stockholders he was the man to run the paper.

There was no question that he impressed the paper's owners. They offered him the fabulous salary of $50,000 a year to run it, but he turned them down. He wanted to own the *New York Times.*

Considering the fact that Ochs's net worth at the time was less than zero, it was a brash thing for him to do. However, at the age of thirty-eight, he was a supersalesman and entrepreneur. Also, despite its excellent reputation, the big newspaper had fallen on hard times. Circulation was down to 9,000, there was a debt outstanding of $300,000, and it was losing $2,500 a week.

One person who had been won over by the Ochs charm was the paper's editor-in-chief, Charles R. Miller, who wielded great influence over its destiny. On learning that rival interests were about to buy the paper with the idea of turning it into a scandal sheet, Miller let it go into bankruptcy.

Ochs worked out an intricate financial plan by which stockholders would receive one share of new stock for each five shares they were holding, and for the floating of two bond issues, with fifteen free shares of stock going to every bond-buyer. Then he clinched his own eventual control of the *Times* by getting together $75,000 to buy bonds in his own name, automatically acquiring 1,125 shares of stock.

He got the money to do this the same way he sold the bonds, by using his persuasive powers to get tough money men on Wall Street to lend it to him. He wrote his wife, Effie, about one stockholder, Jacob Shiff, who, believing his $25,000 in stock to be worthless, gave it all to Ochs.

In 1896 when bankruptcy court put the *Times* on the auction block, Ochs was the only person to make a bid. Five days later he had taken over the publisher's office. He gained controlling interest in 1900.

The next few years were not easy, but this time Ochs profited from past experience. He didn't try any land deals, and he gave every ounce of his energy to making his newspaper a success. He promised to put out a clean newspaper and he came up with the catchy slogan, "All the news that's fit to print," a motto that still appears in a box on the front page. Abhorring the "yellow journalism" of the day, he separated editorial comment from news and insisted on the concept of full-sided impartiality in the presentation of news. He introduced book reviews and a serious Sunday magazine and started printing useful financial news.

Soon Ochs's holdings in the paper were worth a million dollars, and in succeeding years it prospered beyond his own wildest dreams. On several occasions, including a couple of brushes with Tammany Hall, he turned down chances to prosper even more, but he stood by his principles of honesty and fairness. As a result, the paper, while making it financially, also added to its prestige as one of the world's great newspapers.

The newsboy from Knoxville, by way of Chattanooga, had

"advanced confidently in the direction of his dreams," had built a castle in the air, and had truly put a foundation under it.

Robert Allen, Self-taught Genius

Thanks to Mrs. Kathleen Moore, Huntingdon

The story of Robert Allen is both disturbing and inspiring. It is disturbing that he was denied the privilege of attending public school, of being allowed to play and mingle with others his own age while growing up. It is inspiring that, denied all such pleasures and privileges, he educated himself to a degree that is rarely heard of.

Robert Allen was born and grew up in the little town of Rosser in Carroll County. His parents were divorced and his father died before he was born. His mother deserted him when he was six years old.

He was left with older relatives, being brought up by his great uncle and aunt, Eddie and Bevie Jones. The uncle, who was illiterate, did not believe in school, so Robert never went to school. His Aunt Bevie read comics and other stories to him while he was small, instilling in him a desire to read on his own.

In time, he read from the Bible and whatever other books were available in the dilapidated old frame house where he grew up. By the time he was fourteen, Robert had become an able reader. Then one day he discovered the public library. Books became a delight to his starved mind, and also his

Robert Allen, a diamond in the rough.
[Photo by the Commercial Appeal]

best friends. He sought and found the masters of good litera-
ture and devoured the words that they had written. Among
his many readings was the eleven-volume *Story of Civilization*
by Will and Ariel Durant.

Although Robert could easily quote long passages from
Shakespeare, still no one in his home town knew or sus-
pected his ability. Seeing him riding around Huntingdon
with his great-uncle in his old beat-up truck, they saw him
only as the odd person he appeared to be and assumed he
was retarded.

Having been born in 1949, Robert would normally have
been a prime candidate for service in the Vietnam War, but
the military, assuming he was illiterate, did not want him.

Robert Allen grew up some 100 miles in either direction
from Memphis and Nashville, but he didn't visit either of
those large cities. During his first thirty-five years, he never
traveled more than thirty miles from his home. He never left
Carroll County.

He taught himself to play an organ and to pick a banjo,
and during the times when he was not reading, his long,
slender fingers were finding notes on one or the other of the
instruments, allowing him to play the music to the old bal-
lads he had learned.

At the age of thirty, Robert found a job with the Compre-
hensive Employment Training Administration (CETA), a
government program for disadvantaged young people. The
program ended after a year and Robert decided he would
continue his education—not at a public school but at Bethel
College in nearby McKenzie.

Mustering his courage and with nothing more than his
G.E.D. diploma and a twinkle in his soft blue eyes, he presented himself at the enrollment desk at Bethel. Astounded
by his presence—his poorly fitting and mismatched old
clothes—and his request to enter college without previous
schooling, the professors and staff at Bethel nevertheless decided to submit him to a battery of tests.

When they saw his scores, they were even more astonished. The scores were above the ninety-first percentile in the *A* rank and included English, world history, natural science, and the humanities. He not only was accepted at the college, he was allowed to skip his freshman year. Three years later, in 1984, he was graduated—summa cum laude—and when he walked up to receive his diploma he was given a standing ovation by his fellow students and others in attendance.

Vanderbilt University invited him to enroll and continue his postgraduate work there. If there were any who thought Robert wouldn't be able to "cut it" at a major university, they were quickly proven wrong. He made *A*'s and *B*'s consistently and on May 9, 1986, he received his Master's degree in English. He immediately began work on his doctorate in English.

A special salute is in order for Robert—and for Bethel College for discovering a diamond in the rough and polishing it and causing it to shine with even greater brilliance.

Shadrach Madison,
"Free Man of Color"

Thanks to Wylodean and Gene Rogers,
Weakley County, near Skullbone

While "Ole Black Joe," Miss Scarlett's Prissy, Aunt Jemima, and other ante-bellum slaves have often been depicted in songs, books, and movies, little has been documented about black people who were free in the Old South.

Shadrach Madison, property owner and businessman, was such a person in West Tennessee. His story came to light when Gene and Wylodean Rogers of Weakley County decided to research the origin of Shades Crossing (or Bridge) on the south fork of the Obion River. Their quest led them through census records, the minutes of the county court and the circuit court, land grant entry books, register books, and early tax records. The serendipity of their search was a better understanding of the times and how Shadrach Madison fit into them.

Born about 1792 in Virginia, Shadrach (also called Shade) Madison was an early settler in the community of Skullbone who operated a ferry across the Obion River. Court minutes call the river crossing "Shadrach Madison's Ferry" in 1832 and "Shade's Ferry" in 1833. In accordance with Tennessee law, he had registered with the Gibson County court clerk as a "free man of color," and was required to keep a copy of this registration with him at all times.

Census records show that he and his wife, Nulty, were living near this ferry crossing in 1830 with their four children, Sabra (born about 1821), Fielding (1822), Rhoda (1824), and Barilla (1826).

In 1832 Madison was the first person to be indicted in Gibson County for murder. The circuit court minutes give no specifics, except he was found not guilty by a jury two days after the indictment.

Gene and Wylodean Rogers speculate: "He must have been fairly well respected to be able to operate a ferry transporting white people across the river for a fee. Most likely at least a few of his passengers were difficult to collect from; being black made him more subject to abuse than a white person operating the same kind of business. It would seem difficult for Madison not to have had a few clashes. . . ."

Apparently Madison had bought his wife from another slave owner, because in June 1834 he petitioned the Gibson County court to set her and the children free. The court granted this, with Madison being required by law to post a $250 bond. Tennessee law at that time specified that even though a free man of color "owned" his wife by marriage and by deed, the wife, as a slave, was chattel property and could be taken from the owner for payment of debt or for other reasons. Likewise, children of a female slave were also slaves, no matter who their father was. Therefore it was to the family's advantage to obtain Nulty Madison's freedom as soon as possible after modification in 1833 of the law which had required all slaves who were freed to leave the state.

Other restrictions on free blacks included not being a witness against a white person, not voting or holding office, and not visiting slaves without permission of the owners. An 1831 law prohibited free blacks from entering the state for longer than twenty days.

As a ferry operator, Madison was a successful businessman, who saved enough money to become a land owner. He entered land grant claims on several tracts of land near the ferry and eventually was granted a claim by the state on 131 acres. Although Revolutionary War soldiers received free land grants for their service, by this time a land grant entry claim did not give clear title until the grant was issued by the state, often many years after the original claim was made. Cost of the land to the claimer in the 1840s ranged from twelve and one-half cents an acre for rough or hill land to two dollars per acre for the best land. Tax records list Shade Madison's 131 acres as valued at $262 in 1848.

About this time, with restrictions on free blacks becoming more stringent, the Madisons moved to White County, Illinois. Shadrach Madison gave a white neighbor, Thomas B. Murphy, his power of attorney to deed the 131-acre tract of land to Solomon S. Carroll when the land grant was finally received. Murphy closed the transaction in January, 1849. Illinois census records in 1850 list Madison as a farmer there owning land valued at $200, with most of his family living with him.

Where or when Shadrach Madison died is not known, but his name lives on through a bridge in West Tennessee, still called Shades Crossing. And thanks to two devoted historians, the outline of his life's story has been brought forth from dusty records.

Pete Gray,
One-armed Baseball Star

Thanks to Douglas Norman, Knoxville

To a young Tennessean growing up during the Depression, minor league baseball was a reflection of something far, far away. Seeing one of the sixteen major league teams, which were confined to the Northeast and Midwest, was something only dreamed of. Expansion of the major leagues would have been thought rather un-American. There was no televised game of the week. In fact, there was no television. The radio networks broadcast World Series games, but it was not until after World War II that the great growth in the number of local stations led to regular airing of minor league games. Station WKDA in Nashville was one of the first.

It was a long drive to St. Louis or Cincinnati in a day of so-so two-lane roads and no Holiday Inns. Anyone in my hometown who ever had been to the World Series was a local celebrity, in the same class with travelers who had seen the Grand Canyon—real adventurers.

It was therefore a major happening to drive the sixty-five miles from Mount Pleasant to Nashville to see the Vols play.

Along with Chattanooga, Knoxville, and Memphis in Tennessee, Nashville was a member of the AA Southern League. Vol manager Larry Gilbert was considered one of the top baseball men in the country. Through working agreements with different major league teams, notably the Chicago Cubs, and a few good free agents whom he found and signed himself, Gilbert usually had his Vols in contention for a pennant and the annual postseason playoff with the Texas League champion.

Nashville surely had one of the most picturesque of baseball parks, Sulphur Dell, built on the site of a sulphur spring and squeezed into an incredibly small square. Today the famous old dell is a vacant lot in North Nashville at Jackson Street between Fourth and Fifth avenues near the Farmers Market.

The Dell was renowned for its short right field fence, about 250 feet down the foul line from the plate. To prevent too many cheap homers, the fence was built on top of a terrace, known as the "right field dump," and then topped by a high screen. Next to it was an ice house, and prodigious homers were those that cleared the dump, fence, and screen, and landed on top of the neighboring ice house.

This arrangement worked against line drive hitters, but many Vols developed "the Dell stroke," an uppercut swing that looped homers over all the obstacles.

The right fielder stood on a path that ran along the dump at the bottom of the fence. He was so close to first base that some hitters who did not bother to run out singles to right found themselves thrown out at first by the right fielder charging down from his dump—when they charged or moved at all, that is. Gilbert picked up a number of portly oldtimers who could develop the Dell stroke and assigned them to permanent, semi-stationary duty on the path atop the dump.

Many professional baseball players entered the Armed Forces during World War II, giving others of lesser ability a chance to play. One of the most interesting wartime players was Pete Gray, still remembered as the only one-armed person to play professional baseball, first for Memphis in the Southern and then for the old St. Louis Browns in the American League.

Since Memphis and Nashville were big rivals, and in the same league, it meant that people in the Nashville area could enjoy watching Pete play. Pete, of course, was a big box office draw, and on one occasion Nashville had Pete Gray Day to entice even more fans into Sulphur Dell.

Pete aroused great interest. There was much sidewalk discussion among young fans during summer vacation. How did he do it? The consensus usually was that a man with one arm might hit but couldn't field. We were wrong. Pete "made spectacular plays in the field," according to baseball writer Joe Reichler.

Pete hit by choking way up on the bat with his one hand, and he sprayed line drives all over the field. On the bases, he was fast, a league leader in stolen bases, taking big leads off first and standing with legs quivering, ready to go, trying to unnerve the pitcher.

Say what you will about the era and shortage of good players, Pete was a good athlete. He hit a 330-foot homer in Chattanooga and had a .975 fielding average in 1943, with only eight errors.

It was in the outfield that he was really fascinating. He would run under a fly, make a one-handed catch and, almost with the same motion, throw the ball a few feet into the air; tuck his glove under the stump of his right arm; catch the ball with his good hand; and make his infield throw. It was fluid, quick, and done so rapidly that it was hard to follow.

At one point, the league had to make a special ruling on whether Pete committed an error on the catch or throw if he missed grabbing the ball in midair. The league president ruled that the batter was out if Pete caught the ball in his glove, even if he later missed it while changing from his glove hand to throwing hand.

Sulphur Dell has been replaced by the modern Greer Stadium in South Nashville and the Vols by the Nashville Sounds, a member of the Triple A American Association.

Pete played on the 1945 St. Louis Browns team, batted

.218 with fifty-one hits, six doubles and two triples, and he made some spectacular defensive plays. It was good enough to earn him a place in sports history.

His name still comes up, reminding us of the role that minor league baseball played in our growing up, personally and as a state.

In April, 1986, ABC-TV aired the movie, "A Winner Never Quits," the story of Pete Gray, played by Keith Carradine. Before the filming began in Chattanooga in July, 1985, Carradine, 35, spent a month learning to duplicate Gray's glove-to-hand fielding and throwing style with his left hand.

CHAPTER 2

A Funny Thing Happened
. . . in Tennessee

Coffee Comes to the Cumberlands*

Thanks to Mel Tharp, Crossville

In the early part of the nineteenth century, such luxuries as sugar and coffee were unknown or at least not available to the pioneer settlers of the Cumberlands. Their only agent for sweetening was sorghum and there was little of that. Making the syrup was a laborious and impractical process, for the horse-drawn sorghum mill had not yet come into use. The cane had to be chopped and ground or mashed manually. The juice was boiled in kettles and the finished product bore little resemblance to the table molasses of today.

Coffee beans were an unknown entity to most mountain people of that era. It was in the early 1830s when coffee made its first appearance on the plateau. At that time, Crossville was little more than a way station on the old stage road. There were no streets. In winter or during prolonged periods of rainy weather, the area around the trading stores became a morass of mud, horse droppings and urine.

On this particular morning, Dan Knox had come to Crossville to do a bit of trading. His wife had told him to pick up some salt and beans. Upon arriving at the store, Dan was in no hurry to trade, so he decided to browse around and see what kind of things the merchant had in stock. His attention

---

*Published in *Tennessee Folklore Society Bulletin*, March, 1977, and used by permission.

was drawn to a barrel of odd-shaped, chocolate-colored beans.

"What sort of beans air them?" he asked the storekeeper.

"That's coffee, Dan," the storekeeper replied. "They just came in by freight yesterday."

Dan was curious but he wasn't about to reveal his ignorance to the smart aleck storekeeper. "That's jist what I thought they was. I shore been hankering fer a mess of them." It's easy to imagine the storekeeper trying to keep a straight face as he weighed out the beans.

There is no record of how many coffee beans Dan bought, but he must have purchased a sizable amount because he wanted to impress his neighbors. When he arrived home, he told his wife about the new type of beans and told her to get them to cooking while he went around and invited the neighbors. He couldn't wait to arrange to have them come and eat coffee with him. While Dan was out delivering the invitations, his wife started to prepare the beans. She washed them, put them in a kettle, sliced in some fat pork and put them on to boil. The company arrived with fiddles, banjos and dulcimers. The bean dinner took on a festive air.

The fiddles played and the beans boiled. It seemed like the longer they boiled, the tougher they got. Finally, as the story goes, the guests lost patience and Mrs. Knox gave up in despair. No one has any specific knowledge concerning the aftermath but it's reasonable to assume that Dan was the target of some good-natured or maybe not so good-natured bantering for some time afterward.

For Love of Elsie

Thanks to Judith Ann Biddle, Seymour

I have seen a lot of changes in my time with the coming of color television, the calculator, and the computer, but the biggest change of all in my life was back in 1947 when Pa decided we should move away from the city with all its conveniences to a farm in the country.

I remember like it was yesterday when Mama called in our last order to the neighborhood grocery store in the city. She had read off her list and, as was her custom, she finished with the usual, "Put it on Pa's bill." Pa paid that account once a month like clockwork, but this time would be different. Ma continued, "Clyde, figure up our bill and I will pay you when you bring my vittles. We will be moving to the country next weekend." Within the hour, the delivery boy on a bicycle brought the box of food through our front door and right into the kitchen.

We left all that convenience behind when six days later we moved to what seemed another world to me. The farm Pa bought was near Hall's Cross Roads, a mere thirty miles out of Knoxville, but it seemed to take hours to ride that distance.

It wasn't that we had not seen the country before. For the past few months we had grown accustomed to going with Pa and Mama for a regular Sunday afternoon drive in the country, but they had not told us they were house hunting. We only knew that every Sunday, weather permitting, we piled into Pa's old pickup with our picnic basket filled with Mama's fried chicken and potato salad and headed for the country.

Yes sir, we were awfully excited about moving, because we expected it to be a right happy place to live. Pa had told us, "You children will enjoy living in the country. We'll have a big garden and there's an orchard with apple, cherry, peach, and pear trees, grapevines, and a strawberry patch." Up to that time, I had thought one just bought those things at the neighborhood store. "You will enjoy the animals, too," Pa continued. "The farm comes complete with five cows, chickens, a goat, and a pig."

We had never owned any animals before, except for Mickey, our dog, who moved with us. He was more patient than we were that early spring day as we rode piled with the last of our belongings to our new home.

We finally reached the farm, jumped out of the truck, and scattered in all directions to look the place over. Sweet smells of fruit trees gave me my first impression of that farm, but soon the ordinary odor of the country seemed to overpower the aroma of the blossoms and I began to wonder if Pa had made the right decision. The farm seemed overwhelmingly huge then, but I know now that it was small in comparison to those around us.

The truth was, Pa knew how to grow vegetables, but he didn't know any more about animals than we did back then. So, being the wise man that he was, I suppose he knew he ought to start off small.

We kept pretty busy for the first few weeks planting the garden and feeding our chickens and slopping the hog. After a while we settled down to wait for the garden to come up and the trees to bear fruit. Our biggest endeavor then was to learn to entertain ourselves.

No longer did we have friends within hollering distance and since Mama was not used to the things of the country, she quickly made known her reservations about our crossing the pastures and going through the woods to the fishing hole. That left little for us children to do except to look after the welfare of the animals, which we did with a passion. We fed those chickens, slopped that hog, and carried water till we were literally exhausted.

In return we thought the animals ought to be awfully indebted to us, but they weren't. The hens and chickens were always scattered all over the place and ran away when we tried to be friendly to them; the cows were usually so far out in the fields that we never really got to know them very well; and the black billy goat smelled too bad to become a best buddy.

With Elsie the pig it was different from the beginning. She didn't come to us complete with that name, and for the life of me I can't recall why we called her that; but Elsie she became.

Pa put a big empty lard bucket on our screened-in back porch and everything that was not tin, glass, paper, or wood went into that bucket to become Elsie's supper. And she was truly grateful when she saw us kids carrying her bucket of food to her. She would nuzzle up to her gate in eagerness and sometimes we could hardly open it.

We grew fantastically fond of Elsie, partly because she did not put on a front for anybody. She knew we loved her, fat and muddy as she was, and Elsie adored us, we could tell.

One day Pa came to the pig pen as we were pouring Elsie's supper into the trough. "You know, children, we got a big, fat pig on our hands and it's gettin' pretty cold. I think I'll take her to the slaughtering house. We will soon be eating some good old country ham and sausage, children."

We were still trying to figure out what he meant when a few days later he pulled his old Ford pickup right up to Elsie's gate. That's when it struck me! He meant for us to eat Elsie!

Horror of horrors, we could not do that! I admit, being the

oldest child I assumed the role of gang leader at that instant.
I led my sisters and brothers to Elsie's defense, screaming,
"No, Pa! You can't do that! Please, Pa, we ain't gonna eat
Elsie." All of us kids swarmed into the gate and hugged as
much as possible around the rolls of fat we knew as Elsie. It's
a doggoned good thing we did not live near other folks or
I'm sure the authorities would have been there speedily to
see why we were all crying and screaming and yelling as we
tried to push Pa away from our friend.

Pa tried to shoo us aside, and Mama, hearing our blood-
curdling cries, came running to see what was going on. Pa
attempted reasoning with us. "I've bought three more pigs,
children. There will not be enough room in our pen for Elsie
and three more pigs."

He might as well have been talking to the air, for we just
screamed louder.

After a while, Pa, being the kind-hearted man that he was,
allowed us to have our way and backed the pickup away
from Elsie's gate. I figured Mama must have been happy
about the way things turned out when I saw her climbing
into the truck with Pa, her mouth covered with her apron
and stifling her laughter, which was causing tears to flow
down her cheeks.

Elsie lived a long hog's life and finally died of old age. "Or
perhaps obesity," Mama said.

Pa never tried to take another hog to slaughter after that,
but we were fortunate. He met an old farmer named Sam
who smelled a lot like our goat, but who, Pa said, "had a
great love for pigs." Whenever we had three or four hogs that
got too big and fat to keep in our pen, Pa and Sam would
load them up and take them over to Sam's place to live so it
would not be so crowded in our pen.

And in return, Sam was forever bringing us fresh sausage, country hams, pork chops, slabs of bacon, and tender-
loin.

What Mr. Wooten Saw

Thanks to Roger K. Howell, a McNairy County native now living in Columbus, Mississippi

In the community of Cypress near Ramer in southwestern McNairy County, in 1932, the constable appeared to be in a hurry as he drove up to Ernest Wooten's farm house, sending chickens and guineas scrambling from the dusty yard toward the barn lot. Wooten met the tall man on the porch and invited him in, but the officer had more serious things on his mind, explaining that there had been a robbery and that he had a lead on where the stolen goods might be stashed. "I'm going to deputize you," he told Wooten.

Explaining that he had never been involved in law enforcement before, Wooten tried to beg off, but to no avail, and so he got into the constable's Model-T Ford. The long, lanky arm of the law gave the crank a whirl and they were off.

Following the road that led toward the community of Pocahontas, they soon arrived in front of a one-room log house with its front door standing open to welcome any breeze that might wander by. An old man with a long white beard emerged and looked inquiringly at his visitors.

Coming right to the point, the constable said, "We're here to search your house for stolen property."

The elderly farmer replied, "We was just fixin' to set down to dinner. Can you wait till we git through eatin'?"

Nevertheless the officer, with Wooten following closely behind him, strode past the old man and began a search of the premises while the man, his wife, his daughter, and his son-in-law sat at the dinner table glaring at the two intruders who were methodically going through their home.

Suddenly the lawman's eyes discovered a hole in the loft. He told Wooten he would give him a boost to have a look. Wooten scanned the area quickly.

"Nothing here," he reported.

There were beads of sweat on his brow as he dropped to the floor. He could sense an ominous hostility coming from the old man and his family. They knew there was something in the loft, and they were pretty sure that Wooten had seen it.

The search over, the officer and Wooten made their way to the car. As Wooten glanced back over his shoulder, he saw the bearded man reach above the door and take down his double-barreled shotgun. He stood with it in the doorway as the constable cranked up the car and steered toward the bumpy road.

Wooten never told his secret.

What he saw in the farmer's loft was a large, copper moonshine still.

Don't Ye Tetch It*

Thanks to Elizabeth Jones Browning, Knoxville

In the days before Mr. Rockefeller and Congress set the now Smoky Mountain area of the Allegheny Mountains in the Government Park, the state of Tennessee was indeed pioneering in its rural and mountain Health Program. In the assignments of medicos who were staffing these rural centers and locations, young Dr. Tom Bragg Yancey (of Virginia birth) was sent to open a Tennessee Health Center located in Sevierville (with the backing of some state laws as to certain vaccinations, etc.). Dribble by dribble the mountain and rural folk were persuaded to go into this "ferner's" offices for him to tell them about things that they "had had" and that they "had not had." And little by little, the health program was being made effective in this area also.

Dr. Yancey told me this true experience, some years ago, and many years after it occurred.

One afternoon there came into the health center rooms a gangly, raw-boned, ax-faced fellow, of some fifty-years weathering; he sauntered in, chawin' tobacco and all, entering quite non-oral for several minutes. Eventually Dr. Yancey extended a civil greeting and introduction to him, to which

*Published in *Tennessee Folklore Society Bulletin*, June, 1957, and used by permission.

the man responded: "Wall now, Doc, hif hits er tapeworm whut has been a-keepin' me frum work all these yars, don't ye tetch it!"

Git Along, Little Goosie

Thanks to Helen Stewart Conyers, Halls

The Old West had its cattle drives, but there's never been a goose drive to match the one that took place in Crockett County in the early 1900s.

Mrs. Fay Conyers Coffman, age ninety-two, recalls how it happened when her father, Dr. Joe Conyers, went into the goose-raising business in a big way and ended up with 2,000 geese ready for market.

The logical place to take them was to Chicago, and there were rail facilities for the trip at the railroad station at Gates, but that was eight miles away. Dr. Joe decided that the best way to get the geese there was to mount a gigantic goose drive, with farm hands driving the geese along in somewhat the same manner as cowboys escorted herds of cattle along the Old Chisholm Trail. The goose herders, however, did their work on foot, and by all accounts they had their hands full.

Dr. Joe's children also played an important part in the drive. In addition to Fay, there were Frank, Leon, Grover, and Mary. For several weeks before the drive started they fed the geese well so they would be in peak condition. They also painted the heads of the geese red so they could be identified in case any strays wandered off course. Reflecting their temperaments, the geese were given names such as Bossy, Happy, Fussy, and Puny.

Finally the big day came, and the drive began. Soon 2,000 geese were strung out along the road and adjoining fields, honking and squawking their erratic way westward from their starting place four miles west of Maury City.

Occasionally one would take flight long enough to get over a hill, but, all things considered, they conducted themselves fairly well. Some of the geese balked when they came to the Forked Deer River but, after much honking, they finally obeyed their sweating, shooing, shouting handlers and crossed the bridge.

Dr. Joe's children brought up the rear, riding in a gig and picking up exhausted members of the flock who had fallen by the wayside, and then, as Mrs. Coffman put it, "selling them back to Papa."

Apparently there was no "beak count" at the end of the drive, but there were enough survivors for Dr. Joe to have them packed into a freight car and hauled to Chicago. Since there were no passenger cars on the freight train, Dr. Joe, presumably, was allowed to ride in the caboose.

As to profits from his goose sale in Chicago, Mrs. Coffman remembers only that he enjoyed a Fay Templeton performance there, heard her sing "Mary Is a Grand Old Name," and bought the sheet music for the song plus a doll dressed in red satin.

CHAPTER 3

The Blue and the Gray: Tennessee Vignettes

More than any other state, Tennessee was a smaller scale version of the War Between the States. Like the nation itself, the state was sharply divided, geographically and ideologically, with Middle and West Tennessee backing the Confederate cause and East Tennessee the Federals.

When the Secession issue was decided in the legislature, the East Tennesseans were outvoted, and Tennessee officially seceded. That, however, did nothing to change the feelings of those who lived in the eastern part of the state. The schism was manifested in many ways. It meant that brother was sometimes fighting against brother, family against family, and neighbor against neighbor.

Tearing the state apart further was the great number of major battles that were fought on Tennessee soil—Shiloh, Forts Henry and Donelson, Stones River, Chattanooga, Franklin, Nashville—more, in fact, than in any other state except Virginia.

The war affected Tennesseans in another way that was different from other states. As some of the following stories will show, families and neighbors were often drawn closer together, particularly among those who remained loyal to the Union, and sought ways to show their feelings.

The Lieutenant Salutes the Flag

Thanks to Judith Ann Biddle, Seymour

It happened in the little community of Walland in a gap of the Chilhowee Mountains near Maryville. The Civil War was raging and Tennessee had pulled out of the Union to join the Confederacy.

But the mountain folks sympathized with the Union and they let it be known that the Stars and Stripes of the United States would be their flag. A big rally was held and fifteen hundred men from the coves surrounding Walland came out for the raising of the flag.

About this time, units of the Confederate cavalry were scouring the countryside to collect firearms in an attempt to disarm the Union people and thereby secure the safety of all the Confederate sympathizers. In Maryville, a Lieutenant White was ordered to take a detachment of his Confederate soldiers to confiscate the rifles of the men in the mountains. Just as the officer was about to mount his horse, a Judge Wallace, with whom Lieutenant White was boarding, came up and said he had a request to make.

"As you pass up Little River through Chilhowee Gap," the judge said, "you will emerge from the narrow mountain pass between the points of the mountain peaks. There, at the left of the road, you will find the Stars and Stripes floating from a tall pole. Let me ask you not to disturb that flag. The mountain men placed it there. It belongs to them. If you leave it undisturbed, you will be treated kindly on your trip. But, as sure as you touch it or interfere with it, you will have to get out of those mountains."

Lieutenant White said nothing to his men about the judge's warning. As his unit rode through the narrow opening in the mountain, suddenly before them atop a tall pole was the Stars and Stripes floating in all its glory.

Calmly, White halted his troops and then gave a speech he was to remember for the rest of his life.

"Men, that was the flag under which we were born," he said. "It was under that flag our fathers fought and many of them died. While we are fighting under a new flag, still, that was the flag of our fathers. Let us honor it for its history and for the memory of the blood poured out so freely by our brave ancestors in its defense. Instead of doing it injury, I propose that we salute it."

Following the wise lieutenant's leadership, the men rode single file, forming a circle around the pole. One by one they lifted their hats and reverently bowed their heads. Tears unashamedly streamed down the faces of some. Then they rode off by twos to continue their mission.

News of the Confederate men's reverence for that Union flag traveled faster than the men did. Everywhere they went in the East Tennessee mountain country they were treated with the utmost hospitality. The people cooked fine dinners for them, took them into their homes, and afforded them every kindness they could offer, except one.

"They did not bring out their guns and we could not find them," Lieutenant White later wrote.

Little did the lieutenant know that he and his troops almost found the guns in a way they had not imagined. As his men had stood in a circle around the pole where the flag hung, they were encircled in a trap. All it would have taken for hidden triggers to be pulled would have been the slightest insult to that banner above their heads.

The Confederates learned later that their reverence to that old flag of those mountain men had saved them from a bloody ambush.

Jonesborough Rock

Thanks to J. D. Anderson, Elizabethton

Ordinarily, life on a farm in Johnson County in East Tennessee was peaceful, unhurried, and as secure as the Appalachian mountains that surrounded it. One April day, however, the lovely, tranquil scene was deceptive because everyone was either watching or being watched. It was 1864 and the United States was divided by a Civil War.

Young Tom Anderson was one of the watchers. Perched on a boulder on top of the ridge behind the family farm, he had a good view of the Draft Road as it meandered around the hills until it went out of sight behind a bluff overlooking Roan Creek.

There was word through the grapevine that a Confederate patrol was in the area rounding up all able-bodied men to bolster its depleted ranks. Although he was just seven years old, Tom realized the importance of his task—to watch for the Confederates and, if he saw them, to alert his elders.

This War Between the States or, as some called it, "the Brother-Against-Brother War," didn't disturb Johnson County, as far as battles were concerned. This was due, primarily, to its isolated mountainous terrain. Then, too, there were few strategic targets worth the risks. Although Tennessee seceded from the Union in July, 1861, Upper East Tennessee remained loyal to the Union, so most of the boys who left these hills wore blue. Enough wore the gray, however, to cause problems within and between families, and people had to be careful what they said and to whom they said it.

The war had been in progress for almost three years now and men were being consumed by the hundreds of thousands, as many by disease as by cannon and sword. Both sides needed to supplement their depleted ranks. Since East Tennessee had suffered least from the ravages of war, the Confederates surmised, and rightly so, that thousands of able-bodied men were hiding in these hills and valleys, and they determined to find them. The alert, sharp-witted mountain men, however, were not going to be caught off guard and months before had devised a plan.

There were two major land owners in the Draft section of Johnson County, John Anderson and John Dugger. Their farms, of about 400 acres each, adjoined each other along the Draft Road. The plan was to post a lookout on the ridge behind the Anderson farmstead because it offered a view of the road two or three miles down the valley. The men of these farms could be alerted to danger and have time to go into hiding before the danger reached them.

There were dozens of caves scattered throughout these hills, but one in particular seemed best suited for hiding a large number of men. It lay just over the first ridge of Dry Run Mountain on the east ridge of the Anderson farm along the bank of Baker Creek. The entrance was small and protected by an overhanging rock, making it hardly noticeable unless one were standing directly in front of it. Inside, however, the cave opened up into a large room that could easily accommodate twenty or more men. According to the plan, this cave became known as Jonesborough Rock.

Jonesborough, the first capital of the State of Tennessee, was the county seat of Washington County, some sixty miles away from the Draft by the dusty wagon roads. Once a year the farmers of the area would organize a two or three-wagon train and drive to Jonesborough to buy salt, which was as essential as water to these pioneer families. Salt preserved their meats and vegetables, kept their livestock healthy, and flavored their food. The plan was to tell military patrols that the men of the valley had gone to Jonesborough to buy salt. To make the story more believable, only a few days' supply was kept in the barns and houses. The remainder was stored in the cave.

This was the fifth day that young Tom Anderson had been on the ridge. Each day he had notched a small birch that grew out of a crevice in the boulder and there were now five notches in the sweet-smelling bark. Tom had been selected to do the watching because this was planting time and his older brothers and sisters were needed in the fields.

As he looked down to the north side of the farm, he could see and hear the buzz of their activity as they planted corn in the twenty-acre field. It took a lot of corn to feed horses, cattle, pigs, chickens, and eight hard-working people for an entire year. Tom felt somewhat guilty sitting up on the ridge while the others were working, but his father had seen fit to assign him there.

As the sun climbed higher in the April sky, its warm rays began to take their toll, and young Tom became drowsy. Suddenly, he jerked fully awake. There was movement on the road below. A horse and rider crested the hill, then another and another until there were five moving up the Draft Road toward the Anderson and Dugger farms. Rebels!

Tom jumped off the boulder, picked up his cowbell, and raced around the ridge out of sight of the road. Then, according to the plan, he vigorously rang the bell five times, signifying the number of riders approaching. He waited ten seconds and repeated the signal. By this time he could see that his signal had been heard, as his father and brothers in the field began running toward the house. Tom ran down the ridge to join them.

By the time he reached the barnyard, Tom found his entire family gathered there awaiting confirmation of what he had seen. His brother Ezra was sitting bareback on a roan horse ready to dash off to the Dugger farm to alert others there. From this point on, the plan took over. The older boys and their father took some bread and dried meat, along with a muzzle loader, and started on their way to Jonesborough Rock where they would be joined by the Duggers. Their mother, Mildred Anderson, led the girls and the younger children, Tom included, toward the corn field. There was no time to waste. Although it would take the patrol more than thirty minutes to reach the farm, they needed to be in place in the field as though they had been there all morning.

Before they had time to plant one row through the field, the dog Scotty's growl announced the approach of riders on the Draft Road. All activity stopped and the children leaned on their hoes. As the dusty patrol turned into the lane leading to the house, Mildred Anderson cautiously made her way to the gate leading from the field. The captain of the patrol, in a dust-covered, faded uniform, dismounted and slowly walked to the gate to meet her.

"Morning, Ma'am," he drawled as he courteously tipped his hat. "Seems you and these young'uns got a mighty big job to do."

"Well, you're right," Tom's mother replied, "but these are hard times and a body has to do things the hard way."

Even as he talked the captain's eyes were searching for clues. "Now, Ma'am," he continued, "I know you have some men folks on this farm and I would be obliged to you to tell me where they are. I have some business to transact with them."

Mrs. Anderson pushed her bonnet back and wiped her brow with her forearm. "I'm right sorry about that," she replied, "but the men left some time ago to go to Jonesborough for salt. We wuz getting low and you know we have to have salt."

The captain knew that no good farmer would run out of

salt by April and he thought they might have slipped up in
their story. Turning to his men, still in their saddles, he mo-
tioned with his hand an they dismounted.

"I hope you won't mind then, Ma'am, if we have a little
look for ourselves."

Addressing his men again, he directed, "Two of you
search the barn and two check the kitchen and smoke-
house."

Throughout the confrontation, the Anderson children
stood in the field like stone statues. They didn't move a
muscle but their eyes were keenly alert to the whole affair.
The captain removed his gloves and began to beat the dust
from his sleeves and trousers. The horses snorted and
stamped their feet on the gravel. Not many minutes passed
before the searchers returned from their mission.

"Sir, it seems they're telling the truth," a corporal whispered. "We can't find more than a smidgen of salt on the
place."

The captain looked disappointed but he said not a word as
he slowly mounted his horse while his men did likewise.
Reining his horse around, he tipped his hat to Tom's mother,
then looked beyond her toward Tom and said, "Young fella,
tell your Pa the next time he goes for salt to get enough to last
for a year, so's you and your Ma won't have to do the plant-
in'." And without a further word, the patrol galloped off toward the Dugger farm.

Mildred Anderson breathed a sigh of relief as she made
her way back to where she had left off in the row. Picking up
the hoe she looked up at the sun and announced to her children, "It's almost high noon. Let's finish planting these
rows and we'll stop for dinner. Nancy, you take the baby on
in and feed her now." She knew that to leave the field
abruptly would be a dead giveaway if anyone were watching.

After dinner and a short nap time for the small children,
the family went back to work in the field. With the Rebel

patrol in the vicinity they couldn't take any chances. Mildred Anderson knew that, according to the plan, watchful eyes would be trained on the riders until they were completely out of the county, and then word would be passed along that all was clear. Until that time she and the children would have to perform double duty.

Next morning as she was preparing breakfast Mrs. Anderson heard Scotty's bark and, rushing to the window, she saw a lone rider approaching. Only when she recognized him as a neighbor who lived several miles up the valley did she unbolt the door. The rider refused her invitation to dismount for breakfast, saying only that all was clear and that he had more miles to ride.

Mildred Anderson watched him disappear down the Draft Road in a cloud of dust before she bowed her head and said a prayer of thanksgiving. Then she turned to her son, who was coming through the doorway, grabbed him by his shoulders, and half shouted, half sang, "Tom, get yourself to Jonesborough Rock and tell your Pa to bring me some salt if he wants any on his eggs for breakfast!" She watched Tom run out of sight and then announced to the hills, "It's going to be a nice day!"

True to Her Yankee Soldier Man

Thanks to Mrs. Ruth Benson, Knoxville

When the Civil War began, my maternal grandparents were living on a little rocky farm near Ebenezer, about ten miles west of Knoxville. They had three small sons, Vos, Azro, and Homer. Grandpa was a dedicated Union man and Grandma's family was just as loyal to the Confederacy.

Knowing that it would work a real hardship on Grandma and the boys for him to leave, Grandpa stayed on the farm as long as he could; but, finally, to keep from being drafted into the Confederate army, he bade his little family a heartbreaking goodbye and left in the night on a difficult and dangerous journey to Kentucky, where he joined the Union army.

Grandma and the three boys got along somehow, despite all the hardships. Their little house was on a hill above the tracks of the Southern Railway and my Uncle Homer used to tell about how they had a Rebel flag and the Stars and Stripes. Grandma kept a sharp eye up and down the tracks. When groups of the boys in gray went by, her sons got out and waved the Rebel flag while shouting, "Hurrah for the Confederacy." When the blue uniforms were sighted, the Stars and Stripes were waved to the tune of "The Battle Hymn of the Republic." Grandma claimed there was not a word of truth in it, but it made a good story.

A detachment of Union soldiers.
[Photo courtesy of James Hoobler]

Meanwhile, Grandma's father was a prosperous farmer in Louisville, Tennessee, at that time a thriving river port on what is now Lake Loudon. He had a cabinet shop where he kept several slaves busy making furniture and caskets. He had two sons in the Confederate army and felt very bitter toward his Union son-in-law. When the war was at its worst, he wrote Grandma that he was bringing a wagon to take her and the boys back to Louisville. Grandma felt sure he must be getting mellow in his old age and she was happy to be going back to the big old roomy home where she had grown up.

By the time Grandma's father arrived at her house, she and the boys had gathered up their few treasures and a lot of the household goods. It did not take long to load them in the wagon with the three little boys safely atop the load on a big feather bed. When Grandma climbed up on the seat by her father he said to her, "Now, Martha, you realize that this means you are never to see that no-good husband of yours again."

Grandma gave him one scorching glare and said, "Boys, get off the wagon." The four of them, without another word, climbed down, unloaded their belongings, bade her father a not-too-cordial farewell, and stayed on their rocky little farm until Grandpa returned in 1864.

Two more children were born to them after the war, a boy and a girl. In 1900 the girl became my mother.

President Lincoln and the P.O.W.

Thanks to Judge Charles G. Neese, Nashville

Horace Harmon Lurton was one of five Tennesseans to serve on the Supreme Court of the United States. Although he was born (in 1844) in Newport, Kentucky, he joined the Confederate army in Tennessee, was graduated from law school in Tennessee, practiced law in Clarksville, served as a Tennessee chancellor, was elected (in 1886) in Tennessee as a member of its Supreme Court, and was briefly (in 1893) its chief justice.

Between the times he was on the respective highest courts of Tennessee and of the United States, Horace Lurton served on the United States Court of Appeals for the Sixth Circuit. Also on the latter court was Judge William Howard Taft who, after becoming President, appointed Lurton to the federal high court.

During the War Between the States, Lurton attained the rank of major and was taken prisoner twice. The first time he escaped. However, during Morgan's raid in Ohio in 1863, he was captured a second time and imprisoned on Johnson Island in Lake Erie. There he suffered from a chronic lung infection which progressed into tuberculosis in 1865.

Major Lurton's mother visited him in prison, saw his condition, and traveled immediately to the White House to

plead with President Abraham Lincoln to release her son so
he could receive proper medical attention. The President
was sympathetic and agreed to parole Major Lurton "on
leave" from prison for health reasons.

Mrs. Lurton was appreciative but argued to the President
that the time necessary to process the parole would be too
long to salvage his health. She pleaded to be allowed to take
her son home with her at once to begin his treatment. Again,
the President was understanding. He wrote out in longhand
his famous order to prison custodians:

Let the boy go home with his mother.
A. Lincoln

The Free State of Scott Rejoins Tennessee

Thanks to Ellis O. Butler, Oneida

Most Tennesseans have heard of the "lost" state of Franklin but only recently were they reminded that there was also a "Free and Independent State of Scott."

That's the name that was adopted by Scott County when it "seceded" from the state 125 years ago at the outbreak of the War Between the States. Tennessee had voted to secede from the Union and join the Confederacy, and so Scott County, a hotbed for Union loyalists, decided to secede from Tennessee. The county court of Scott was called into special session and its members voted unanimously to declare their independence and set up their own free and independent state.

Ellis O. Butler of Oneida writes: "The brave squires dispatched a messenger to Nashville to inform the governor and the state legislature that the former Scott County was now independent and no longer a part of Tennessee but, unlike the rest of Tennessee, still a loyal part of the United States of America."

Quickly responding to such insubordination, the Confederates ordered a military force to march against Scott County and to arrest the rebellious squires and take them into custody. But the squires got word of the approaching troops, hid out, and managed to evade capture.

With the end of the war, Tennessee in 1866 rejoined the Union but Scott took its time about applying for readmission to the state of Tennessee—125 years to be exact.

On March 17, 1986, the county court adopted a resolution recommending that "The Free and Independent State of Scott" be dissolved and that "petition be made to the governor and legislature of Tennessee for readmission into the state of Tennessee as Scott County."

It was explained that since 1986 was the year of Tennessee Homecoming, the people of Scott, "in a spirit of forgiveness," had decided to declare their own free state "duly dissolved and disbanded."

No doubt also influenced by Homecoming '86, the Tennessee legislature, shortly before its adjournment in May, 1986, adopted a resolution sponsored by state Senator Anna Belle Clement O'Brien welcoming the return of the lost county.

It should be noted that during its years of "estrangement" Scott never refused tax monies from the state, nor was the state bashful in collecting taxes from the citizens of Scott (aka Scott County). Thus the action by the people of Scott was, unlike that of the Lost State of Franklin, symbolic only. That's a good thing for a number of reasons, among them the fact that this arrangement allowed Tennessee to claim one of the nation's best senators, Howard Baker, Jr., and a mighty fine congressman, his father, Howard Baker, Sr. Their hometown is Huntsville, county seat of Scott County.

CHAPTER 4
Fantasy and Facts . . . in Tennessee

The Wampus Cat

Thanks to Nan N. Badgett,
Tucson, Arizona

During the early 1920s in our small community near Cades Cove in Blount County, the word spread that a Wampus Cat was abroad in our land. No one ever actually saw it firsthand, but it was supposed to chase cattle, kill sheep, and could even whip a big coon hound.

Along about dusk, we would hear a shotgun blast, and soon men would pass down the road in front of our house, walking, on horseback, and in T-Model Fords, all prominently displaying double-barreled shotguns or Winchester repeaters. They were off to see the Wampus Cat.

Many years later I asked a senior citizen who lived in the community in the earlier days to tell me about the Wampus Cat. His watery eyes sparkled, and with a grin he said:

"That was back in the days of National Prohibition. We purely invented the Wampus Cat to have an excuse to get out of the house. When one of the boys got a hold of a jar of better-than-ordinary moonshine liquor, he would fire a signal shot. Then we would all gather in the basement of Brown's Grocery Store to share his good fortune. We needed to make no explanations to leave home. When the signal shot was heard and a man grabbed his gun, his wife knowed he was off to hunt the Wampus Cat."

Tales My Grandmother Told Me*

The following account, told to me by my grandmother and verified by other members of the family, is supposedly a true happening concerning the strange behavior of an ancient family clock at the death of my grandfather.

This particular clock, handed down from generation to generation for over a hundred years, was a large, wooden-framed affair with a long pendulum which swung rhythmically to and fro, insuring perfect time to the second.

The numerous engravings on the glass face, the delicate hand carving on the wooden parts, and the old-style Roman numeral lettering on the dial gave the clock an unforgettable, stately quality.

It had been given to my grandfather by his father, and at my grandfather's death was supposed to be given to one of his sons, who in turn would hand it on down to one of his male children. This, according to the legend of the clock, was the only way of acquiring ownership—that it be handed down from father to son.

It so happened that none of my grandfather's children wanted the clock—in fact none of them would take it. The

---

*From the collection of E. G. Rogers and contributed by Earl Lockmiller of Athens, Tennessee, under the above title. The reader will see the similarity of this legend to the folk-music version of "Grandfather's Clock." This was published in *Tennessee Folklore Society Bulletin*, June, 1951, and used by permission.

situation stood thus at the last illness of my grandfather in 1924.

While lying on his deathbed he again tried to persuade one of his two sons to take the clock, care for it, and carry on the tradition. Neither would consent to take it.

On January 16, 1924, he called for a change in his will. At the stroke of midnight, on this same day, he started drawing his last breath. As this ancient clock began tolling the twelfth hour, his life began ebbing slowly away. When the clock had tolled twelve times, my grandfather was still fighting for breath—*but the clock did not stop striking.* It continued to strike until he had drawn his last breath. The clock had struck twenty-four times—then completely stopped running.

Later, at the reading of the will, it was learned that the change he had made was that his wife was to keep the clock. Coincidence? Maybe. Here is a chain of mysterious events: his death came the day the will was changed—the clock had never been known to strike more than twelve times—it stopped at the very second of his passing away, although fully wound—it has never run since his death—all these facts cause one to wonder where to draw the line between coincidence, unexplicable events, and superstitious belief. At any rate, it is a strange occurrence.

Great Jumping Bullfrogs!

Thanks to Mrs. Victor G. Conley, Newcomb

A young girl was out hoeing corn on a farm near Newcomb one day when she became thirsty and went to a nearby spring for a drink of water. She lay down to drink when suddenly she leaped up. Something was jumping inside her! She was sure she must have swallowed one of the bullfrogs that lived near the spring!

Running home clutching her stomach, she blurted out to her mother that she had swallowed a frog. Immediately her mother sent for the family doctor who examined her and then confided to her anxious parents, "It's just her imagination."

But the girl only yelled louder. So her parents sent for an herb doctor who lived nearby. After patiently listening to the girl's story, he looked at her very seriously and said he could tell she was telling the truth and that he had "just the medicine you need to get rid of that jumping frog." However, he would have to go back to his office to get it.

"Please hurry," the girl pleaded.

At his office, which was also his home, the herb doctor got out a supply of emetic, a medicine that causes vomiting. Then on the way back to the girl's house, he stopped at a small creek and caught a bullfrog, which he put in his pocket.

As soon as the girl drank the medicine she began coughing up everything that had been in her stomach. At just the right time the doctor reached into his pocket, dropped the frog at the girl's feet, and announced, "There it is! You've coughed it up!"

The patient got well immediately and with a big smile said, "I told you I swallowed a bullfrog." Then she went back to the corn.

Phantom in the Memphis Orpheum

Thanks to Doug Morris, Metro Editor
of the Knoxville Journal

Mary is a twelve-year-old girl and she always sits in Row C, Seat 5, in the Orpheum Theater in Memphis. The unusual thing about this is that Mary died in 1921. Mary is a ghost.

Vincent Astor, building supervisor, organist, and historian, explained that Mary is "just a little girl who lives in the theater" at the corner of Main and Beale.

According to Astor, Mary "likes the crowds, the lights, the make-believe. She has been described consistently as being a girl of about twelve, with brown braided hair, white dress, and long, black stockings." Nor do you have to take only Astor's word for it.

"Dozens of people have seen her," he explained. "I never have, but I've felt the strange, cold feeling when she is around. I believe in her myself, or else I wouldn't be making a fool of myself telling you this. People I trust have reported seeing her. She's shy, but she makes little noises and does mischievous things. But she has no malice. There's nothing gory or spooky about her."

Astor said there is a "curiosity" about Mary in Memphis. "I've had people tell me I'm crazy, quote the Bible to me, say they are scared and aren't coming back. But Mary holds my credibility. I know for a fact she is here. In fact, I'm rather fond of her."

Orpheum Theatre, home of a twelve-year-old girl's ghost.
[Photo courtesy of Orpheum Theatre, Vincent Astor, Historian]

Astor tells of the time in 1972 when he was in the balcony changing a light bulb. "I had a feeling someone was looking over my shoulder. I looked. There was no one there. Then I felt that cold, eerie feeling many have described. It was like getting into a bathtub of cold liver. Once you feel it you'll never forget it."

Technicians working late at night in the magnificent old, domed building have reported hearing her muffled footsteps in all sections of the supposedly deserted theater. Dressing room doors slam backstage. The ethereal image of her white dress has been seen darting through the dark halls and roaming the uppermost aisles of the balcony. People strolling by the theater at night have heard from within the distinct sounds of a girl crying.

Performers at the theater over the past half century have noticed a little girl in what looks like a white school uniform sitting in seat C-5 in the box nearest the stage. The New York company of *Fiddler on the Roof*, when playing the Orpheum in 1977, became certain the theater was home for a ghost and held a seance there after the opening performance.

A Memphis State parapsychology class investigated Mary, using seances and a Ouija board. Class members reported that they learned that Mary died in a falling accident that had nothing to do with the theater.

Why is this school girl drawn to the Orpheum? Other theaters have sometimes reported to be homes to resident ghosts, usually people intimately connected with the stage. The casts of Nashville's Circle Theater, for instance, used to report "feeling" the presence of Walter Bauer, a long-time artist-member and guiding spirit of the community playhouse.

Could Mary have had aspirations for the stage? Could America have lost a future star of the magnitude of Helen Hayes in the long-ago accident? Does Mary weep for what might have been?

Ghost in the Cemetery

Thanks to Beverly Askew, Newport

The year was 1924 and I was sixteen years old. I had been married for two years and had a son, William, Jr., who was eight months old.

We lived near Cosby in Cocke County and in those days people helped each other out in times of sickness and other troubles. It happened that Mindy Gunter, a good friend of the family, was seriously ill and people were needed to take turns sitting up with her.

To get to her house, I had to walk several miles and go through an old family cemetery. Since babysitters were unheard of in those days, I took my little boy with me. There were no cars and to have taken a horse and buggy would have meant following a bumpy, circuitous road, adding miles and hours to the already long trip. So I walked to Mindy's house, carrying William in my arms.

We reached Mindy's house well before dark and I took a turn sitting with her. As the evening wore on, other people came, including a young man who had had too much to drink. He started flirting with me and wouldn't stop.

Since others had come to help out, I decided to take William and start the walk back home, slipping out the back of the house so the drunk wouldn't see me.

It was past midnight as we started through the woods and pretty soon we came to the cemetery. Suddenly I saw the strangest sight I had ever laid eyes on—something standing by one of the graves, about five feet high, and glowing all over!

He—or it—was right in my path and there were briars on either side, so there was no way to go around it.

I considered returning to Mindy's house but the thought of the drunk back there was enough to rule out that idea. I stood there hoping the ghost would go away. He didn't. He just stood there and glowed.

Then, getting up all the courage I could muster, I decided to run up to it and give it a swift kick. With William under one arm and the other ready to do battle if necessary, I ran and kicked as hard as I could.

As I swung one foot at it, my other foot slipped out from under me. That thing flew all to pieces and I fell screaming, while William started yelling at the top of his lungs.

Then I took off running as hard as I could. I didn't look back. I was afraid it might be gaining on me.

The next day my husband went out to the cemetery, hoping to solve the mystery. My "ghost," he said, was an old rotten tree stump filled with foxfire.

Even though that explanation was reasonable, I didn't walk back to Mindy's for a long time.

The Moonshine Still Ghost*

Thanks to Ruth W. O'Dell, Newport

Cocke County has never been noted for many "still ghosts," and it has not even one "ghost still"—however, a moonshiner will run from a "still ghost" even faster than from any "Revenuer." Here is a true ghost tale told to me by the son of the Methodist Circuit Rider who did not even believe in ghosts.

Back in the early days of our moonshining industry, we had government stills and often our young men would congregate in certain places and go in a body to some nearby still on any "gut-letting Saturday night" that suited their fancy. After a while they would return in high glee singing and swinging along our mountain trails, often telling ghost tales (which, of course, made them more or less ghost conscious) until finally one night the entire crowd saw a ghost sitting on a stump in a sort of low place. It frightened them terribly, and those who could run did so. They ran like the wind. Many times they saw this ghost in this same place.

A young Circuit Rider who knew the boys and hated to see them partaking of the spirits of fermentum decided he would let them see a real sure-enough ghost. Consequently he spent some time preparing a ghostly headdress, then he

---

*Published in *Tennessee Folklore Society Bulletin*, September, 1954, and used by permission.

wrapped himself in sheets and waited in the woods where the boys had complained of seeing the ghost each Saturday night. When the preacher heard the boys returning from the still, he mounted a stump, waving his ghostly arms. The boys stopped "stock-still" in a body, so frightened they could not speak for a moment. Then one screamed out, "Lord have mercy, look! There's two of them tonight." This time they ran like lightning—greased at that!

The preacher looked around behind him and there sat the other one. The preacher began screaming for the boys to wait, and by the time he overtook them he'd torn off his ghostly apparel. Never did the boys know he was the worst frightened of any of them, but willing to have been in order to stop the boys from visiting the still.

CHAPTER 5
The Way It Was:
Yesteryear in Tennessee

Christmas at Ozone

Thanks to Freelan E. Lewis, Crossville

My story of a very special Christmas seventy years ago when I was eight years old begins with an old-timey two-room school which was housed in the Presbyterian church in Ozone. We were always furnished two teachers—one well on in age and the other just out of school. This particular year the older professor had a beautiful sixteen-year-old daughter who had all the boys, my fifteen-year-old brother included, wild with fantasy and jealousy, each vying for her affection.

Money was hard to come by, about the only sources of income being from the coal mines or work in timber. My father made crossties for the Tennessee Central Railroad. These sold in three grades delivered for 90 cents, $1.00, and $1.10.

Christmas was getting close, and none of us had any spending money. My brother rushed home from school each afternoon to help Father make crossties. Both of them wanted to earn enough to buy presents for the family, but then they learned that the buyer would not arrive until after New Year's. This was crushing news.

The Christmas excitement was saved when my oldest brother, who was away in another town working, sent Father $20 and my brother $5. This was all my brother needed to compete with the other guys for the affection of "The Girl."

On Christmas Eve, shortly before Ozone's annual Christmas tree social was to take place (the church then, as now, serving as the locale for community affairs), my brother asked me to go with him to the country store.

"What do you want most?" he asked me.

I told him a cap pistol, but it cost $1.50. The doll our little sister Frances craved cost $2.50 with an extra dress. Brother looked longingly at the big red box of candy I knew he wanted to get for "The Girl," but then bought the gun and some caps, the doll and dress, and with the $1.00 he had left, he bought a pretty handkerchief for Mother. He glanced at the box of candy again, and then we started back home.

On the way I thought about what he had done, and I think I loved him more than anybody else in the world. I wanted to do something. But what?

Finally I decided to go to "The Girl" and tell her what I knew. When she answered my knock, I blurted out how Brother wanted to give her that big red box of candy but that he loved Frances and me so much he had spent all his money on us.

That night at the Christmas tree, presents were being passed around and "The Girl" was getting gifts from all the fellows. Then a beautiful package was handed to Brother. On the card, "The Girl" had written: "My father gives you permission to walk me home."

For seventy Christmases I have been able to visualize the love I saw in my brother's face when he decided to give everything to his family. Even now when I visit the little Presbyterian church that was also our two-room school and social house, I get the tingles.

It was a very special Christmas for me that year in Ozone.

Piano in the Ditch

Thanks to Josephine Neel Wallen, Murfreesboro

When my mother consented to marry a farmer, she said, "Bob, if I marry you, will you promise to move my mother's old square rosewood piano from Winchester to the farm?"

Mister Bob, as his friends called him, solemnly promised that he would do so, even though the farm to which he would take his bride was far back in the roller-coaster hills of Middle Tennessee above the Duck River in another county, a long, tedious journey over rutted roads during the horse and buggy days.

So it was that the ponderous old piano, wrapped in quilts and bedded down in straw, was hauled in a two-horse wagon to the lamp-lit parlor where the womenfolk had arranged the plush furniture to make way for the "big square."

To gather in the parlor and sing the beautiful old hymns, camp meeting songs, the melodies of Stephen Foster, and the popular favorites of the day grew to be a regular family custom. The hearty sessions were more than the old square was equal to, and before long it was sounding like a tin pan. Something had to be done. In those days families had to entertain themselves.

My mother summoned a man from one of the piano houses in Nashville, hoping he could restore the sweet tone of the old piano. However, he gently broke the news that the old square could not be restored. Before the piano man left, however, he had an order for a new upright to be shipped to Normandy, six river-winding miles from the farm. In spite of having to cross the river and climb a steep mile-long hill where the road hung like a great tilted shelf over a deep ravine, this was the route chosen for the piano. Oddly enough, the piano man had been brought to the farm over the longer, more level route from Tullahoma. It may have been that the family felt that the city man's insides were more delicate and finely tuned than those of the newly purchased upright.

Once again, Mr. Bob had to haul a piano over what in those days served as a road. Fortunately, the river was low when he and the hired men crossed it, but the hill was as high and rough as ever. It was a hill up which a buggy would have to stop to give the horse a chance to rest. Many a load of hay, stacked too high, had toppled over and landed in the wide-mouthed, narrow-bottomed ravine. But a piano was different from a load of hay, Mr. Bob claimed. Besides, there was no stopping a woman who had her head set on a new piano.

When they reached the hill, the men scotched the wagon wheels and talked to and patted the sweating mules, telling them they had a big job to do. The unwieldy crate that enclosed the piano was difficult to anchor with ropes and slid back and forth and rocked from side to side in the wagon-bed. The men tried to brace it as much as possible.

After another rest, the mules were pulling harder and climbing faster when the wagon tilted sharply and the crated piano skidded with such momentum that it dived over the side of the wagon and slid to the bottom of the ravine, its fall broken somewhat by some bushes.

Men and mules stared in shocked silence at the piano in the ditch. What the men said after the first shock subsided was not fit for the ears of the mules, who knew instinctively that what had happened was much worse than a spilled load of hay. The unspoken thought was who would break the news to my mother?

Approaching darkness gave the men an idea. The weary, hungry mules, if unhitched from the wagon, would plod straight to the barn gate, where they would foretell the calamity in a more eloquent and apologetic way than the men ever could have.

By morning, news of the catastrophe had spread throughout the countryside. A crowd of men, women, and children gathered on the hillside to see the remains of the piano hoisted from the ditch.

After much discussion as to the best means of getting the piano out, the bushes above the piano were cut and the steep sides of the gorge were lined with long, slick, freshly cut poles that served as a sort of smooth track. Then the strongest men, equipped with ropes, chains, crowbars, and other tools, went down into the ditch, and after much toiling, heaving, and lifting on their part, and with much "geeing" and "hawing" on the part of the mules, the crated piano was pulled out of the gorge.

When the piano in its battered crate was at last heaved onto the wagon, the journey was resumed with greatest caution. The crowd of onlookers followed, speculating on the condition of the piano.

The damaged crate was eventually deposited on the front porch of the farm house and pried open. To everyone's amazement, the piano, save for a few scratches and dents, was all in one piece. After running a few scales up and down the keyboard, my mother struck the chords of a familiar hymn, and the crowd took up the song, rejoicing with her, to the strains of "Oh Happy Day"!

Box Supper in the Tennessee Hills

Thanks to Josephine Neel Wallen, Murfreesboro

A generation or more ago, a box supper was one of the few ways of raising money in the rural schools of Tennessee. It was always a big occasion for the people of the community, especially the young girls who packed and decorated their boxes with the hope that the boy they had their eye on would outbid the others and be the one with whom they would share their goodies.

Because transportation and communication facilities were limited in those times, many romances and marriages occurred among couples in the same or nearby communities. And these box suppers often revealed who was "sparking" whom. At other times there was heated competition among rival bidders.

One of these box suppers had an auctioneer who fancied himself somewhat of a poet and often delivered his hypnotic chant in rhyme, making it easy to recall. One of his doggerels was:

> Come on, boys! Step right up! Don't act quare
> If you wanta eat with a damsel fair;
> Come on, boys! The next 'possum, coon, or fox

Box suppers were important occasions for people living in small communities.

[Photo courtesy of Mrs. Harrison (Anne) Crawford]

You ketch will more'n pay for this here box;
Come on, boys! Step right up and make your bid!
There's no way of telling what's hid
In this here fancy thing I'm a-holdin';
Right now, I smell chicken, brown and golden;
And I'd swear I got a whiff of chess pies!
Come on, boys! Buy it! Look into her eyes.
Tell her how much you dote on and admire
The way she can cook a tender fryer;
Come on, boys! Speak up—don't be bashful;
Make the ladies think you're from Nashful;
Come on, boys! A man's bound to do his part;
What's money, boys, when a purty girl's heart
Is all tied up in a box with ribbon?
And, 'pon my word, I ain't a-fibbin';
Come on, boys! What'm I give? What'm I give?
One dollar I hear! As shore as I live!
She's goin, boys! She's gone! Now, aintcha sorry
You didn't buy it, even if you had to borry?

A Visit to Aunt Nolie's in Sweetwater

Thanks to Linda Morton Norton, Gatlinburg

One of my favorite childhood memories deals with the many visits we made to my Aunt Nolie's house in Sweetwater for Sunday dinner. Daddy would pull up in front of her house and park the car along the curb beside a bank covered with green grass and creeping phlox.

Aunt Nolie and all the aunts and uncles and cousins would run out to greet us, kissing Daddy, Mama, and all of us kids. Aunt Nolie raised Daddy when he was a little boy after his mother had died and she still persisted in calling him "Sugar."

After Aunt Nolie had settled us on the front porch swing, she and her daughter, Aunt Aline, would hurry to the kitchen to prepare Sunday dinner. Aunt Nolie made the smoothest little round biscuits, so light, while Aunt Aline's specialty was cornbread. I can never make my biscuits so smooth, try as I may.

Uncle Conner would go out to the chicken yard and after carefully choosing a nice fat rooster, he would grab him and wring his neck. I remember the chicken running around flapping his wings with his head off and then, finally, falling to the ground. He gave up ever so slowly but he did make a delicious meal.

Sunday dinner—what a delight—served in the screened-in wellhouse with a cool, cool concrete floor! Uncle Conner ate with us kids after the other grownups and our parents had finished their meal. He was a big man with red, shining skin and bright blue eyes that I thought twinkled just at me. He had the most beautiful smile.

I watched with rounded eyes as Uncle Conner took a slab of whipped butter that was congealed in a huge green crockery bowl, placed the butter on one of Aunt Nolie's smooth biscuits, and popped the whole thing in his mouth at once.

Dear, dear Uncle Conner, a big strong farmer, who would lean down and really communicate with little children! I believe he was a child himself.

Aunt Nolie and Aunt Aline were always dressed to the nines, in the height of fashion, wearing silk and crepe housedresses, ever so immaculate, combed, and perfumed. I always wondered, did they get up out of bed like that? And Aunt Nolie, when going out, used a fancy walking cane and her shoulders were draped with a red fox stole. These lovely aunts were so prim, so sophisticated, and so beautiful. We'd sit on the front porch, swinging, while Aunt Nolie told us stories about her late husband, "Mr. Harrell."

Years later after I'd grown up and was married and living in Alabama, I'd stop by to see Aunt Nolie, Uncle Conner, and Aunt Aline on my way home to Tennessee to see Mother and Daddy. I'd proudly show them my babies and they'd kiss and "sugar" me. If we drove by late at night, too late to stop, we'd toot our car horn and Aunt Nolie would always know it was me. My Aunt Nolie was a fine lady, a product of Tennessee, born and bred, and now returned to the soil of her native land that birthed her.

Would Blue Cross
Pay for These?

Long before the days of packaged antibiotics and trauma centers, people depended on folk cures and herb remedies for the things that ailed them—from a touch of flu to mad dog bites.

In many rural areas, people became so attached to their herb doctors and other medicine men that they swore by them even after modern medical facilities became available.

Today it is well known that many ancient, natural remedies had a scientific basis for their curative powers. We use reserpine, the juice of the rauwolfia plant, to treat hypertension; digitalis, from foxglove, for heart disease; and ground-up hog pancreas in production of insulin for diabetes.

Many—probably most—of the "cures" were of no value whatsoever, but it would be difficult to persuade some of the hundreds who swore by various concoctions put together by their favorite medicine men.

Consider the experience of Arthur Herman Richardson of Burns, who died in 1980 at the age of eighty-four, after carrying on a lifetime practice as an herb doctor. He treated anyone who needed him, regardless of whether the patient could pay. It was said that he did so much good with his old-fashioned remedies over the years that testimony from his thousands of patients could fill volumes.

Charles J. Rochelle of Gordonsville and his madstone.
[Photo courtesy of Tom Normand, Staff Writer, *Nashville Banner*]

According to his daughter, Mrs. Kathryn Daugherty, he used methods taught him by an old Indian doctor, Chief Eagle Feather. She remembers watching him leave home with his medicine kit (a diaper bag) on foot or on muleback to go help someone who was ailing. "He helped so many people," she said, "money or no money. He would be a millionaire if everybody had paid him."

Mr. Richardson had only a first-grade education, but his wife, the former Dovie Miller, taught him to read and write, and he learned Latin and shorthand himself.

He gathered and dug, washed and dried, and concocted his remedies from the herbs and roots himself. When the demand for his services grew, he started ordering some ingredients from an Indiana botanical garden.

Apparently Mr. Richardson's cures worked for himself, too, for, his daughter recalled, he was "never sick in his whole life except one time he had a fever."

Then there was Walter F. "Pookes" Baker who, at the age of four, was told by his grandmother that he was blessed with the rare folk gift of healing the thrush, a troublesome childhood mouth infection.

According to the legend handed down for many generations, when a baby is born after his father dies, as happened in Baker's case, he has the magic ability to cure thrush by simply blowing three times into the victim's mouth.

Thus, at a tender age, young Baker, who lived in Gallatin, found himself the object of desperate parents who would bring their sick babies for him to cure. Over a period of fifty years, he estimated that he had cured more than 2,000 cases.

He recalled one instance when a mother "took the baby in, had it on a pillow. It was nothing but skin and bones. I blowed in the baby's mouth. I didn't see her for two months. I asked how the baby was doing and she said just fine."

Baker said that, according to reports from parents, every child he had ever tried to heal had gotten well—within three days.

Turning to one of his lighter episodes, he recalled: "There was a couple come to my house. She was a very beautiful woman. And I blowed in her child's mouth, and she said, 'I think I've got the thrush.' And my wife said, 'No, grown people don't have it.' My wife was jealous of her, wouldn't let me blow in her mouth."

Apparently the theory about this particular type of "curing" was fairly widespread. A list of folk remedies by Ruth W. O'Dell of Newport included this item: "To cure thrash (note the different spelling) let a person who has never seen his own father blow in the child's mouth."

Ms. O'Dell's list also included a cure for snakebite, namely: "For snakebite, especially a copperhead snake, catch a toad-frog, and while it is still alive, jerk it in two and place over the wound. It will draw the poison out quickly; if this is impossible, cover the wound with salt."

A more dramatic cure for snake bite is told in an article in the *Nashville Banner* by staff writer Tom Normand. It is called the madstone cure, a madstone being a rock that is formed in the stomach of a deer. In Colonial times, according to the article, pioneers and Indians claimed that the victim of a mad dog bite would apply the madstone to draw out the poison (note the similarity to the toad-frog remedy in the O'Dell list).

Normand's story was accompanied by a picture of Charles J. Rochelle of Gordonsville, who had acquired one of the objects at a junk sale in Alexandria.

A detailed explanation was given of just how the madstone works: "The infected area or the place where the bite occurred is scraped and the stone is applied. It clings to that area, drawing out poison until it is full, then drops off. The stone is then immersed in a basin of milk. There the poison flows from it in the form of a green liquid. The stone is reapplied until it no longer clings to the body—meaning no more poison in the bloodstream."

Sounds convincing, all right, but maybe if you are so unfortunate as to be bitten by a rabid animal you should follow a licensed physician's advice and take shots, painful though they may be. Besides, it is very unlikely that Blue Cross would take kindly to the listing of a madstone on a major medical pharmacy claim.

Here are a few more of the O'Dell "cures":

• To relieve a bad cold, drink burned whiskey. Put a flannel cloth on the chest after greasing the cloth with tallow and sprinkling it with equal parts of a mixture made of turpentine, lamp oil, and camphor. Take a hot foot-bath and go to bed.

• To relieve rheumatism, boil wild-cherry bark and drink the tea. If this fails, make pokeberry wine and drink it. (No doubt lots of rheumatism victims found it necessary to take the alternative remedy).

• Liquor in which rock candy is crushed is effective for a cold or a sore throat.

• For insect stings, apply tobacco juice.

• To relieve congestion of the chest cavity, make a mixture of turpentine, lamp oil, and camphor mixed in a base of mutton tallow. Apply to a flannel cloth and heap upon the chest.

A Miracle Named Elvis

Thanks to Estelle Broadrick, Cross Plains

When Lydia Josephine Cook delivered her first baby in 1910 at her home in Robertson County, her doctor made house calls and was there for the delivery. But the doctor's presence wasn't enough, as he immediately perceived that little Elvis Cook was very weak and there seemed little chance he would survive the night.

In those days there was no "angel van" or helicopter transport to rush an infant to an incubator in a children's intensive care ward. In fact, there was no hospital anywhere in the area. But there was a service that turned out to be just as good. Although the doctor had another urgent call to make, several miles down the road in his buggy, he advised the worried father to send for the baby's grandmother, Mrs. Lou McNeely, daughter of the best midwife the doctor had ever known.

Upon arrival, Mrs. McNeely took one look at the baby's feeble efforts to live, the flame of life so weak and flickering, turned to the father, Marshall Cook, and ordered him to "go somewhere and get a bottle of good whiskey."

Quickly saddling their horses, Marshall and his father, Bert Cook, galloped away to the home of the local bootlegger (the county was dry). Although the bootlegger was known to haul whiskey out from Nashville, he was also known to be very selective about to whom he sold the illegal merchandise. The elder Mr. Cook, not a regular customer, explained the circumstances to him. The bootlegger was unimpressed. The story sounded pretty farfetched to him. He figured them to be agents of the law.

Finally, Mr. Cook said, "I give you my word as a gentleman, if you will sell us a bottle of whiskey, before I will let you get into trouble over this sale, I will sell my farm."

A man's word was as good as his bond in those parts, and so the two men were soon heading back to the Cook place, the bottle tucked securely under Marshall Cook's arm.

When they arrived the grandmother grabbed the bottle, poured some whiskey into a cup, and warmed it with a little hot water. She held baby Elvis on her knees on a blanket before the opened door of the woodburning range, and bathed his "joints" with the warm whiskey solution.

Then she directed someone to mix a little hot water with whiskey and sweeten it with sugar. Dipping a clean cloth into the toddy, she put the folded, dripping cloth to the baby's mouth. Now and then she would turn the child to the warmth of the oven's breath, then she would bathe him again with the whiskey solution. Time went by slowly and everyone was silent, each busy with desperate prayers.

The clock hands drew close to midnight and they were reminded of the doctor's last words before departing: "There will probably be a change around midnight. He will revive or he will cease struggling. I will make my other calls and will be back early in the morning."

Just as the old grandfather clock struck the first chime proclaiming the hour of change, the baby stirred. As if it were a signal he had waited for, he turned his head as though searching for his mother.

"Lydia, get ready for him. He is hungry," the grandmother cried, and as the young mother folded her arms around him she was laughing with tears running down her cheeks.

As he had promised, the doctor returned in the early hours of the morning. He was amazed. "Mrs. McNeely literally snatched that baby from death," he declared. "Truthfully, I had no hope he would live the night.

During the ensuing years both the doctor and the grandmother told the story many times of "a miracle named Elvis."

In the spring of 1986, Estelle Broadrock wrote that Elvis Cash, her first cousin, then in his mid-70s, had been "strong and healthy" almost his entire life.

CHAPTER 6
Happenings in Tennessee

Jeff Howell's Buryin'*

Thanks to C. Hodge Mathes

It was the strangest funeral ever held in Galax Cove. Two groups of mourners glowered at each other across the open grave. Behind them at a little distance an outer circle of mountain neighbors huddled nervously in the rustic churchyard.

In the center of each of the two inner groups sobbed a young woman holding a babe at her breast.

The strange thing about it was that each of the two women knew herself to be the wife of Jeff Howell, whose body was even now being lowered into the grave. And each knew Jeff Howell was the father of her babe.

The dead man's father and mother and a score of kinsmen stood grim-faced beside Louviny, whom all Galax had seen married to Jeff by Preacher Pleas Ballard. Louviny's tears rolled unrestrained down her cheeks, some of them raining upon the face of her now fatherless child.

The other woman, too, was surrounded by a bodyguard, strangers all in Galax, who had come with her bringing Jeff's body across Big Piney from the lumber camp on Nolichucky, where Jeff had been working and where he had been killed in a sawmill accident.

---

*Published in *Tennessee Folklore Society Bulletin*, May, 1940, and used by permission.

"This here's Minnie, yer son's woman, and his baby, an' I'm her uncle," the oldest of the Nolichucky cortège had abruptly announced when the wagons had brought the corpse and the sad tidings to the parental cabin.

There had ensued a stormy scene, of course, with angry threats and counter-threats, as another age-old "triangle" was pieced out, with its fifty-mile base-line stretched across the mountain divide and its apex—well, that was lying out there in a wagon, in a crude pine coffin.

"Hit won't never do to let them two women git together, or they'll be hell a-poppin' all over the place," the cooler heads had cautioned, and Minnie had been hurried away to a neighbor's house for the night. The rest of the Nolichucky folk had likewise been provided lodgings as far as possible from the house of mourning.

Even at that, there were muttered hints of a "ruction." The keening of the women at the "wake" that night was made more harrowing by the forebodings of mothers, sisters, and wives over what was likely to happen at the burying on the morrow.

Soon after daybreak they sent a horse and buggy to the head of the creek to bring Preacher Pleas Ballard. He was the patriarch, priest, and prophet of Galax Cove. Ninety years of age, stone-blind, and all but bedfast with palsy, he was seldom seen in the valley any more, but when there was trouble, when the shadow of fear fell over the dark mountain slopes, they always sent for Preacher Pleas.

He had come again today. They carried him in his chair and placed him near the head of the grave, and he sat leaning upon his gnarled staff, his sightless eyes blinking in the afternoon sun.

When the plowlines with which the coffin was lowered had been pulled up, coiled, and laid aside, a few spadefuls of clods rattled down upon the covering-boards, and then the crowd stood with bared heads.

Nothing broke the stillness save the weeping of Louviny

and Minnie, but the air was surcharged with impending tragedy. On both sides of the waiting grave hardset jaws, and cold, unblinking eyes seemed only waiting for a signal. At any moment either woman, bursting out in a bitter accusation or angry challenge, might give that signal.

"All ready, Uncle Pleas," someone whispered.

Pleas Ballard could neither read nor write, but when he prayed it was as if he conversed with One who stood and listened. He knew no "Thou" nor "Thee" but addressed the Almighty respectfully as one gentleman might another.

Pleas Ballard prayed.

"We're here, Sir, to bury a pore boy we thought a heap of. A nice young man he was, Sir, an' we're sorry he had to go so suddent. We hate it mighty bad he didn't allus do the right thing. The last time I seed him, about a month ago, I reckon, he come up an' told me about the sorry mess he'd got his self an' two good weemen into. He was jest a pore weak mountain boy, Sir, an' he was sufferin' a livin' hell.

"We hope he got it fixed up with you, Sir, afore he was took. But we want you to take pity on these here two young weemen with their babes. Hit's human nater fer 'em to be full of hate an' pizen feelins agin each other. You know how that is, Sir. But what's been done can't be undone, an' we want ye to help 'em fergit an' fergive. Them's two mighty sweet words, Sir, they air. Help these pore young widder women to fergive him that's dead, an' fergive each other. Thanky, Sir. Amen!"

The menfolk put on their hats again, the outer circle moved softly inward, and the two groups at the graveside had somehow melted into one, with silent shaking of hands all round.

Louviny and Minnie meanwhile edged closer, as all the men took turns shoveling the earth into the grave.

Suddenly, in an ancient symbolism of the hill country, each woman, without a word, held out her own babe to the other and for a brief moment clasped the other woman's child to her own bared breast, marble-white against the folds of her "mourning dress."

Louviny was the first to speak.

"If ye'll come an' take the night with me, Minnie, I'll be right proud to have ye."

Mr. Mulberry Saves the Day

Thanks to Elizabeth Smith, Clinton

When I was growing up in the '20s near Bulls Gap in Hawkins County, it was our hired man, Mr. Mulberry, who taught us to bury early harvest apples in the hot clay banks for quick ripening. He also showed us where the "kill-dees" nested to hatch their perfect little eggs, buff colored with freckles, that were pointed on one end so the wind wouldn't roll them out of the croppings of crumbling limestone rocks on the high hills. We marveled to see the little birds run up and down instead of hopping like other birds. When we got too close to a nest, the mother would pretend to be crippled, with one wing dragging, to lure us away. Everything Mr. Mulberry did was fun. He even made bringing home the cows an adventure rather than a chore.

My fondest recollection of Mr. Mulberry was the day we moved from one farm to another three miles away. My brother Sam had a collection of cats and when the movers came, the cats scattered, and so we had to leave them behind. For Sam, the excitement of moving was overshadowed by the fact that his cats, including one special calico named "Friendly Cat," were not with us.

After we reached the new farm, Mr. Mulberry, noticing Sam's tears, inquired. "Why is the little fellow crying?"

"It's his cats," my mother said. "They ran and hid and the men couldn't wait."

Mr. Mulberry nodded and walked away without another word, to complete his chores. When he had finished, he reappeared and asked, "Do you mind if I borrow one of them burlap bags in the barn?"

The moving finished, the tired little family rested on the front porch with the light from a kerosene lamp shining through the window, listening to the click of the katydids from the darkened yard.

"Who will give the cats their drinks of water?" Sam whispered. Before my father could retort, a noise stopped him. Someone was approaching, whistling. Heavy shoes crunched on gravel.

"Who's there?"

"Mulberry."

Mr. Mulberry came into the circle of soft light from the lamp. He carried a writhing, meowing bag.

Sam looked at Mother, speechless.

"Now stand back, boy. These cats are mad and mean. They've fought me every step of the way."

Mr. Mulberry opened the bag and cats ran in all directions.

Seeing the dour look on Father's face, Mr. Mulberry lifted his hat to Mother and said, "Them cats will be worth their weight in gold around here. The mice got into Mr. Moore's wheat something awful last year."

Then he turned to Sam, "Take good care of them mousers, boy."

With a wink Mr. Mulberry was on his way home, rubbing his back where needle-sharp claws had ripped his skin. He had worked all day with the movers, done his chores with the animals, then walked three miles to catch the cats and three miles back again to our new home.

Several years later, one evening after coming home from high school, I was sent to pick the last grapes of the season before the yellow jackets got them all. As I worked I heard the pounding of the hammers of men roofing the barn. Mr.

Mulberry had come out of semi-retirement to help, although Father had tried to talk him out of it. My basket was nearly full when I heard Mr. Mulberry begin to sing, "When the roll is called up yonder, When the roll is called up yonder, I'll be there."

Then cries, feet pounding down the hill to the house, voices yelling, "Get pillows! Get pillows! Mr. Mulberry is hurt!"

"Hurt bad?"

"He fell through the roof."

Our dear friend had come a good piece of our childhood with us. We must travel the rest of the way without him.

Tennessee's Sleeping Beauty

Thanks to Ruby Nevil Covington, Cross Plains

Tennessee's sleeping beauty didn't equal the feat of the fairy-tale princess who lay asleep in her castle for 100 years before being awakened by the kiss of a prince, but she was real and she did sleep for twenty-four years.

Susan Caroline Godsey was born in 1836 in Gibson County. When she was seven her family moved to Obion County, settling in the community of Woodland Mills, twelve miles northwest of Union City.

According to family members and acquaintances, "Susie" was as healthy as most children up to her eighth year, when she "took the chills," which she had off and on for two years. Then, while visiting a sister who lived several miles away, she had another chill and a doctor who had recently moved to the area was called in.

The family later learned that he was a quack, after he had left town in a hurry. But when he took care of Susie he administered several debilitating potions to the poor girl. His "remedies" included sulphuric ether and "phium," described by another doctor as "enough to kill any three men."

For three years thereafter, Susie had twisting, cramping spells. Then as quickly as they came, they disappeared and she settled into a sleep that, despite frequent waking periods, kept her in bed until her death twenty-four years later at the age of thirty-seven.

The search for a physician who might be able to help her went nationwide and beyond. A physician came from Paris, France, to see her, requiring the services of an interpreter to communicate with her relatives. His only accomplishment, however, was to satisfy his curiosity as to the truth of what he had heard.

In 1867, her brother, B. W. Godsey, her brother-in-law, James Jurney, and her niece, Zenoba Jurney, took her to Nashville, where for several days under the care of a well-known physician named Dr. Robert Eve, she attracted intense interest among medical students. Her great beauty no doubt added to the intrigue, for she had continued to grow and develop despite her illness.

But the efforts of Dr. Eve in Nashville and those of physicians at a medical college in St. Louis three years later were to no avail. An article that first appeared eighty-five years ago in the *Union City Commercial* reported that "while in that city celebrated physicians from all parts of the country came to see her but her case baffled the skill of them all."

In a typical twenty-four-hour cycle, it was said, she would awaken each morning at six and each hour thereafter until noon. In the afternoon she would wake up at three, "at sunset," then at nine and eleven at night. Her waking periods would last from five to seven minutes, and during those times doctors and relatives would do their best to keep her awake, telling her of the pretty things they were going to bring her, but to no avail.

The *Commercial* article, which was reprinted in the *Union City Daily Messenger* thirty-five years later, said: "Her sleep was more the appearance of death than a peaceful slumber. There was no sign of life. A mirror held to her nose and mouth exhibited not the slightest blur of moisture upon it. The lightest, filmiest down laid upon her nostrils would not be agitated."

Circus and carnival operators became interested, among them P. T. Barnum, who made Susie's parents several attractive propositions, one amounting to $1,000 a week, if they would allow him to exhibit their daughter to the world.

Despite their humble circumstances, the Godseys turned down all such offers, and when they died the estate left their children amounted to only a few acres of land.

Near the end of her twenty-four-year sleep, Susan Godsey began to take a slow turn for the better. People found that for the first time they could wake her from her slumber during times other than her usual wakings. The effects of the drugs were apparently beginning to wear off, but it was too late. Her tired body had had all it could stand and she quietly passed away, not from an illness, but from the quack doctor's "remedies."

Millard Fillmore Buchanan

Thanks to Doug Morris, Metro Editor of the
Knoxville Journal

It happened on a mountain farm twelve miles west of Rogersville, around the turn of the century.

Millard Fillmore Buchanan arose one morning and told his wife, Barsha Locke Buchanan, that he was going to the store to sell his horse.

He left his saddle in her keeping, headed down the road, then turned and rode back up to the cabin. He bent down from his horse to where Barsha stood in the doorway and kissed her. He handed her his rifle and rode away.

Barsha never saw him again. During the ensuing thirty years before her death, she lived alone. But some said that in her mind, at least, he was always there.

She always set a place at the table for Millard at every meal.

She cared for his saddle, taking it with her when she went away from home for fear it would be stolen or damaged.

She burned a kerosene lamp in the window all night, every night.

The clothes he had left on a chair the night before he went away were never disturbed except when she occasionally washed them.

A nail in the door where a shaving mirror had hung was never allowed to be moved.

Earl "Boast" Gladson of Nubbin Ridge Road in Hawkins County recalls that he used to live in the same hollow as Barsha when he was a boy and many times he drove her to town in his horsedrawn wagon.

Recalling those days, he said, "Nobody knows for sure what happened to Millard Fillmore Buchanan, but I know this, Barsha looked for him at every meal."

During the years after he left, stories circulated around the mountain community concerning what happened. One was that when he arrived at the store where he was to have sold his horse he was met by a woman and they rode away into Kentucky.

He was said to have dropped the name Buchanan, going as Millard Fillmore.

According to another story Buchanan was jailed in Virginia and Barsha packed food and sent it to him by William A. "Ance" Hawkins, a neighbor of Barsha's. (Hawkins was a great-grandfather of Morris Shanks, retired Rogersville banker who became intrigued with the story of Barsha's thirty-year vigil and provided many of the details of the story as it is known today.) Hawkins was said to have encouraged Buchanan to return to Barsha, but that Buchanan refused because of the unworthiness of his past actions.

If that indeed was the case, Millard Fillmore Buchanan greatly underestimated the love that his wife Barsha held for him. Whatever misdeed he may have done, Barsha would have forgiven him in less time than it would take to say "Millard Fillmore Buchanan."

The First Funeral of Bush Breazeale

Thanks to Deloris Jo Stafford, Harriman

On June 16, 1938, seventy-four-year-old Felix "Uncle Bush" Breazeale drew national attention, becoming Roane County's most famous citizen. On that hot Sunday afternoon, he attended his own funeral and listened while his eulogy was delivered.

People came from across the nation for the event, hailed as the largest rural gatherings ever to have occurred at that time in Tennessee. The highly publicized "funeral" was scheduled for 2:00 P.M. but by 9:00 A.M. more than a thousand "mourners" had already assembled, the crowd gathering outside the small, wooden Cave Creek Baptist Church, near Kingston.

As the morning and early afternoon wore on, cars, trucks, and buses continued to arrive, filling every available field and barnyard. By the time the "funeral" began, an estimated crowd of 8,000 had assembled. Cars doubleparked along the narrow dirt road leading to the church created a mammoth traffic jam, delaying the arrival of the "funeral cortege" for forty minutes. While state highway patrolmen worked to clear a path for the procession, a carnival-like atmosphere prevailed. Concession stands dispensed cold drinks and sandwiches as everyone eagerly awaited his first glimpse of the "living corpse."

The cortege finally arrived, led by an undertaker from

Felix "Uncle Bush" Breazeale standing by his coffin.
[Photo courtesy of The Harriman Record]

Loudon who was in charge of the service, with several press cars following him. Then came the hearse, with the "deceased" seated beside the driver. In the back rode the black walnut casket built by Uncle Bush himself.

The eager mob surged forward to look, and once again officers worked frantically to clear a way for the "pallbearers" to carry the empty coffin to its place in front of the congregation.

Uncle Bush, his long whiskers neatly combed, followed the "pallbearers" and sat beside the casket as the service began. Gospel groups from Knoxville, Kingston, and Chattanooga provided music. Fred Berry of Knoxville sang a solo. The Reverend Charles E. Jackson, former pastor of the Rockwood Christian Church, had come from Paris, Illinois, to deliver the sermon.

Repeated requests for quiet were ignored by the excited congregation, and the *Roane County Banner* gave this description of Uncle Bush: "Calm as a September morn, he sat in front of the preacher. A slight smile played around his lips. Not seeing the crowd his eyes lifted up to search the blue beyond the top of a giant oak tree. His eyes held something that wasn't in the faces of the crowd around him."

The idea for his own funeral had come to Uncle Bush several years earlier after he started to make a coffin. He told reporters that "boughten" caskets were cheaply constructed and he wanted a good one. The boards he selected were cut from trees that grew on his farm in the community of Dogwood. While he labored over his coffin, he thought of its intended purpose, and he began to wonder what his funeral service would be like. Soon he was consumed by an intense desire to see that the service was conducted in what he considered to be the right manner, and that the facts of his life were "correctly set out."

Years before, he had been charged with murder, though later the charges were dropped. Uncle Bush had never married, and his explanation was, "I couldn't have the woman I wanted and I never wanted the women I could have." Since he had no descendants to see to matters after his death he began to make his own arrangements.

Local papers discovered his plans and publicized them. When people read of the strange event about to take place, they wanted to have a part in it. A Knoxville funeral home took the handmade casket and lined it. Area businessmen sponsored a trip to Knoxville, about forty miles distant, where Uncle Bush was squired around the big city and was fitted for a new suit. Florists from Knoxville, Lenoir City, and Chattanooga donated floral arrangements (they were stripped bare after the service by souvenir hunters).

At the conclusion of the "funeral" service, Uncle Bush moved among the crowd shaking hands and signing—with an X—the programs that had been printed for the occasion.

Hours after the conclusion of the service, the crowd finally dispersed and Uncle Bush took his handmade coffin to return to his farm alone.

In the weeks that followed, "Roane County's most publicized citizen" was in constant demand. He rode in local parades, made personal appearances at theaters, and appeared on Robert Ripley's *Believe It Or Not* radio program. He was also featured in an illustrated article in *Life* magazine.

On February 9, 1943, Felix Breazeale died. At his request, only a song and a prayer were used at the simple graveside service, as Uncle Bush was laid to his final rest in his polished, handmade coffin.

CHAPTER 7

Politics, Tennessee Style

The Night They Moved the Courthouse

Thanks to Rebel C. Forrester, Obion County Historian, Union City

At 3:00 A.M. on July 9, 1890, the blasts of a shotgun startled the sleeping pigeons in downtown Union City. In response to the signal, two hundred prominent citizens and businessmen gathered at the intersection of First and Church. They brought their guns and wagons. Their mission was to go to the Obion County seat of Troy twelve miles distant, enter the courthouse, remove the county records, and bring them to a new courthouse that stood ready and waiting in Union City. They were about to change the county seat from Troy to Union City. This action, although legal, produced bitter feelings which still linger to this day.

Davy Crockett had taken time out from bear hunting in the Obion bottoms to help his friends lay out the county seat of Troy on March 16, 1825. The bears were gone now and the Indians had long since ceased to hunt in the game-rich lands around nearby Reelfoot Lake. The earthquakes which had created the lake in 1812 had returned in 1832 to damage the courthouse in Troy, but the movement underway that hot July night was to shake its foundations in a more meaningful and powerful way.

When the Civil War had burst upon Obion County, Troy

Obion County Courthouse, Union City, Tennessee.
[Photo courtesy of the Tennessee State Library and Archives]

was a prosperous, growing community. However, the winds of change had already begun to blow. Twelve miles north, the small hamlet of Union City, founded in 1854, was taking shape. Its name and reason for being were based on the rail junction there.

Rail officials had offered to bring their line to Troy if some inducement were given. However, the people of Troy had declined, feeling that the town's importance as the county seat would cause the railroad to come there anyway. The projected railroad was moved away from the city, and Troy's leaders made an urgent appeal for the line to be built as originally planned. Rail officials were said to have replied that there were "two places they wouldn't go, Hell and Troy!" Thus the line bypassed the city and was moved northward toward what would become the site of Union City.

After the tides of the Civil War had receded, the rails brought new growth to Union City. The rail cars brought the latest frocks, suits, cookstoves, and farm equipment. They also brought immigrants, who added a new energy to the excitement of a growing city. Troy merchants found their trade slipping away.

As might be expected, there were those in Union City who disliked the twelve-mile ride to Troy for necessary legal business. A branch law court had been set up in Union City in 1869 for city affairs, but if a person had county business, he had to use a full day for a trip to Troy and back.

When Charles N. Gibbs, son of the founder of Union City, went to Nashville in 1870 as a delegate to the Constitutional Convention, he successfully pressed an amendment (Article X, Section 4) to the new constitution excepting Obion and Cocke counties from requiring that two-thirds of the voters approve a change of county seat. A simple majority could make the change. For several years, no efforts were made to move the county seat.

Union City continued to grow, and in early July, 1888, work began on a grand $18,000 courthouse in the town, bonds having been issued by the city for its construction. On January 1, 1889, the structure was officially deeded to the county, provided the county seat was changed. In February, the mayor and board of aldermen moved their offices into the courthouse, offering its use to the branch law court and chancery.

Union City's next move took place in the county court. A petition was presented calling for an election to settle the issue by majority vote. Troy adherents were forced to yield as the court voted twenty-two to eleven to call an election for May 18.

Then a hard-fought and bitter battle began in earnest. Union City forces circulated a newspaper called the *Issue*. They offered to give the people of Troy their own law court if they would agree to the change.

Troy citizens were outraged at the prospect of losing the county seat and at the newspaper's attacks against prominent citizens of their city. However, they seem not to have replied in kind, at least in print. Their own press issued a mild-mannered, sober appeal called the *Golden Rule*, which argued logically for the retention of the county seat in the geographic center of the county.

While the newspapers battled it out, the people attended many public debates. The well-organized Union City forces presented Will Griffin, editor of their city's newspaper, the *Obion Democrat*. He was cultured and shrewd but no match for the forceful Joe Dean, influential member of the county court.

Finally, election day came, May 18, 1889. When the votes were counted, it was found that Union City had won by 3,455 to 1,906, two votes being cast for the small town of Rives. The margin of victory was just over one hundred votes short of a two-thirds majority, but, thanks to the constitutional amendment, only a majority was needed. Troy citizens protested that many who had voted in Union City had been in their graves since the Civil War.

The issue then moved into the courts, as the Troy forces obtained an injunction in Chancery Court to prevent the election results from being presented to the court. The Chancery Court dismissed the suit in October, but attorneys carried the matter to the Tennessee Supreme Court, where it was dismissed again in April of 1890. Finally election results were brought before the Obion County Court on July 7.

In what must have been a stormy session, the results were approved by a vote of twenty-one to twelve. A committee was appointed to remove the records "as soon as practical" and to carry them to Union City, "placing them in the offices which have been prepared for them."

But as the removal committee departed to go about its work, Troy attorneys filed a last-minute injunction in Chancery Court to stop the removal. Court had adjourned, but the chairman of the court added to the court minutes the information concerning the injunction and stated that court was dissolved.

It remains unclear whether or not the removal committee received word of the injunction. If they did, they chose to ignore it, assuming that it would be dismissed. Union City's patience was worn thin and plans were completed on Tuesday to remove the records.

The men who assembled in downtown Union City on the early morning of July 9 were determined to end the stand-off peaceably, but they were armed. They did not want a confrontation and discreetly timed their arrival in Troy for early morning. As they rode along, they stopped everyone they met, allowing no one to contact Troy and give the alarm.

When they stopped to re-group on a hill just above their destination, Joe Temple, who worked for the telephone company, climbed a telephone pole and called officials in Troy, giving them notice that they were coming after the records. The persons contacted may have assumed, of course, that the call came from Union City, giving them the impression that they had time to organize to prevent the action.

The group from Union City moved quickly into Troy, through the quiet streets and toward the old courthouse. The door was open. Entering the courthouse, they found that the county records were secured in a locked room. After a brief debate, a Mr. Johnson volunteered to break down the door if someone would lend him a horse to get away.

Bud Adams offered his high-spirited black, the act was quickly carried out, and Mr. Johnson sped away, stopping in Union City only long enough to change horses before continuing across the state line into Kentucky to avoid prosecution.

The men brought out the large and heavy county record books, placed them in the wagons, and turned their teams toward Union City, the new county seat. There is no record of confrontation, and it appears the military-like maneuver was, as later reported to the court, conducted in a "peaceable and orderly manner."

The arrival of the men in Union City was no doubt attended by a large crowd, who had by this time heard of the bold maneuver. Cheers rang out as the wagons rolled into the downtown area and the sweaty but triumphant warriors unloaded the records, officially launching the city in its new role as county seat.

When Chancery Court met, the injunction was annulled, since it is said to have read that the records should remain "where they now are," a statement which the Union City attorneys no longer had cause to protest. Court met for the first time in the new Union City courthouse on August 4, 1890.

The unfortunate misjudgment made by those in Troy which resulted in the loss of the railroad and the consequent development of Union City to the disadvantage of Troy had finally had its ultimate consequences. Union City continued its growth and moved into the future.

Those who fought over the bitter issue have long since passed from the scene, but there are yet those who will not forget the night they moved the courthouse.

Who Tore Jim Norvell's Coat? *

Thanks to Maggie J. Lowe, Murfreesboro

The following incident occurred during the memorable presidential campaign of 1844. The Whigs, who were opposed to the admission of Texas, nominated Henry Clay; the Democrats, who were in favor of its admission, supported James Knox Polk of Tennessee.

There was a great rally held in Murfreesboro, and people attended from far and near. Each side had its followers. Douglas Brown fiddled for the Whigs, and Jim Norvell fiddled for the Democrats. Late in the afternoon, the rally ended in a free-for-all fight between the opposing parties. In those days it was considered a dishonor to fight with anything but your fist. So when the riot ended there was no serious damage done except that Jim Norvell's long-tail coat was badly torn.

Some braggart laid down the challenge, far and wide, that he could whip the man who tore Jim Norvell's coat. In what

---

*Maggie Lowe says she is indebted to J. W. Lowe, her father, for this story. She has since discovered that Chip Henderson gives a different version of it in *The History of Murfreesboro.* However, at the time her father gave her the story, he had never read Mr. Henderson's version. Ms. Lowe's father has lived near Gum, Tennessee, all of his life and was well acquainted with the descendants of Carroll Wooten. This story was published in *Tennessee Folklore Society Bulletin,* June, 1954, and is used by permission.

is now the Gum neighborhood, there lived a man by the name of Carroll Wooten who was known throughout the countryside as champion of all who indulged in the fistic arts. Now, this was not hard to understand for Carroll was almost a giant in size.

Someone who knew of Carroll's reputation as a pugilist persuaded him to go to the braggart and say that he tore Jim Norvell's coat. Carroll finally agreed. When the braggart saw the giant that stood before him, his fighting spirit wilted. Carroll calmly stated that he tore the coat and inquired of the braggart what he wanted to do about it. After the braggart surveyed this enormous man, he replied, "I have nothing to say, Carroll, except that you tore a hell of a slit in it."

The election was held, and Clay carried Polk's own state, but Polk went to the White House. But the question ever asked and never answered is, "Who tore Jim Norvell's coat?"

The Battle of Athens

Thanks to Doug Morris, Metro Editor of the **Knoxville Journal**

When President Reagan visited Athens in 1985, a resident of the McMinn County seat remarked that there hadn't been so much excitement since "the Battle of Athens."

What happened at the Battle of Athens on that day in August, 1946, sounds like the concoction of a movie script-writer devising a scene for a Wild West "shoot 'em up" with the forces of law and order represented by indignant citizens who took up their guns and ousted an entrenched political machine.

Doug Morris, Metro City Editor of the *Knoxville Journal*, wrote:

Nationwide attention was focused on Athens . . . during the greatest violence and bloodshed in Tennessee election history. Outgrowths of that battle included: Some 20 people wounded, but there were no fatalities; 14 automobiles overturned and burned in or near the town square; the county jail was struck by a fusillade of gunfire and dynamite; 25 deputies jailed; Sheriff Pat Mansfield and State Senator Paul Cantrell fled the county.

The uprising was led by former GIs, recently returned from World War II, in which they had fought for freedom, who contended they were being denied free elections and honest government.

The GIs were backing a fusion ticket composed of Republicans and Democrats against the McMinn County powers. Bad blood had been building during the days preceding the election, with the GIs claiming their people were being arrested by the score and jailed on trumped up charges. On election day the GIs posted their people at the polling places to see that fairness prevailed.

The trouble began when poll watcher Ed Vestal was thrown through a glass door. The GIs took matters in their own hands, joined by some of the town's leading citizens. They went to their homes for pistols, shotguns, and sticks.

Although the incumbents' forces had been swelled by additional deputies brought in from neighboring cities and counties, they were no match for the hundreds of irate citizens. Sheriff Mansfield, State Senator Cantrell, and a number of others escaped the net and fled the county. Some twenty-five others took refuge in the jail.

The GI forces and other citizens laid siege to the jail at 8:00 P.M., and eight hours later, the "ins" came out with their hands up. Some in the crowd yelled, "Hang 'em, hang 'em," but the revolutionists had a better plan. They took them to the edge of town and removed their clothing so that, as one of them put it, "they wouldn't come back."

George Wood, McMinn County election commissioner and speaker of the state House of Representatives, conceded victory to the GI ticket in a telephone hookup between Athens and Nashville, with Safety Director Lynn Bomar as witness. The victorious ticket consisted of a sheriff, trustee, register of deeds, circuit court clerk, and county court clerk. All were veterans of World War II except one, who was a World War I veteran. There were three Democrats and two Republicans.

The citizens set up a three-man provisional government to take over the county and city in the absence of those who had been put out. Two years later a county council form of government, one of the first in the state, was created.

The Battle of Athens is history now. It happened at a time when there were no voter registrations and no voting machines. Now the scars have healed and Athens has blossomed into a modern, growing city with more than double the population of 7,000 it had in 1946.

A sign on the outskirts of the city describes it best. It says, "Athens—The Friendly City."

Mother Knew Best

Thanks to Mary Glenn Hearne of the Nashville Room, Nashville Public Library

The fight for women's suffrage covered a period of seventy-two years. It was waged in the halls of Congress and in all the forty-eight states, but final victory came with Tennessee's vote. And the victory in Tennessee came with the casting of one deciding vote by a young Tennessee legislator, Harry T. Burn of Athens.

The nineteenth amendment to the Constitution, giving women the right to vote, was approved by a two-thirds vote of the Sixty-sixth Congress on June 4, 1919; however, that was just the beginning of the biggest battle of all, the state-by-state campaign to achieve the needed ratification by three-fourth's majority, or thirty-six of the states.

Leading the ratification effort was the National American Woman Suffrage Association, headquartered in New York City and headed by Carrie Chapman Catt. In opposition were the National Association Opposed to Woman Suffrage (for ladies) and the American Constitutional League (for gentlemen).

The sixty-year-old Mrs. Catt, carrying on in the tradition of Elizabeth Cady Stanton and Susan B. Anthony, began firing off telegrams to all the governors asking them to call special sessions of their legislatures to obtain ratification. She also sent messages to all the forty-eight state suffrage auxiliaries.

On August 9, 1920, Tennessee became the thirty-sixth state to ratify the nineteenth amendment.
[Photo courtesy of the Tennessee State Library and Archives]

The "Suffs," as they were called, went into action, meeting with party leaders and getting pledges of support among legislators. Equally active were the "Antis," who visited state capitals, warning governors and legislators that woman's suffrage would lead to socialism, free love, and the breakup of the American family.

By January 1, 1920, twenty-two states had ratified the constitutional amendment, and by February 16, the birthday of Susan B. Anthony, ten more fell in line. Mrs. Anthony, who had written the suffrage amendment first introduced in Congress in 1878, died in 1906—after each succeeding Congress up to then had defeated it.

Now, only four more states' approval was needed and the crescendo of the battle grew. Oklahoma ratified the amendment on February 27, but only after Miss Aloysius Larch-Miller, a young suffragist, had gotten out of a sickbed to debate the issue with a leading antisuffragist, and then died just two days later. On March 10, West Virginia became the thirty-fourth state to ratify and Washington state ratified on March 22.

The Suffs then turned to Tennessee in search of what cartoonists called their "perfect 36." The pressure was turned on the state's Governor Albert H. Roberts, along with its legislators from Memphis to Bristol. Because Governor Roberts was in a campaign for reelection, he didn't want to rock the boat by calling an extra session on the hot-potato issue of women's suffrage.

People in high places, including President Woodrow Wilson, former United States Supreme Court Justice Charles Evans Hughes, and Tennessee Senator Kenneth McKellar, urged him to call the special session. Antisuffragists in the state bombarded him with requests to delay the call and some threatened him with defeat in the primary if he did call it. In something of a compromise, Roberts announced on June 28 that he would convene the assembly on August 9, four days after the August 5 primary.

It was a time of wild cheering, but suffrage leaders, both
national and state, knew the fight was just beginning. Mrs.
Catherine Tatey Kenny, Chairman of Ratification for the Tennessee League of Women Voters, opened a Ratification Headquarters at the old Maxwell House Hotel while the Antis, under the leadership of Miss Josephine Pearson, of Monteagle,
set up their headquarters in the Hermitage Hotel. Later, both
sides would operate from the Hermitage.

Mrs. Catt, who had been on the scene since mid-July,
would later write in her book *Woman Suffrage and Politics:*

> The Southern summer heat was merciless and many legisla-
> tors lived in remote villages or on farms miles from any
> town. Yet the women trailed these legislators, by train, by
> motor, by wagons and on foot, often in great discomfort, and
> frequently at considerable expense to themselves. They
> went without meals, were drenched in unexpected rains,
> and met with "tire troubles," yet no woman faltered . . . .

A key leader in the Suffragist fight was Anne Dudley of
Nashville, wife of Guilford Dudley, Sr. She had served as the
first president of the Nashville Equal Suffrage League from
1911 to 1915. She became president of the Tennessee Equal
Suffrage League in 1915 and the third vice-president of the
National American Woman Suffrage League in 1917.

Answering Governor Roberts's call, the legislators
swarmed into Nashville August 9 for the special session to
consider ratification. As they alighted from trains that
brought them, they were greeted by ladies of both persuasions, who "sweet-talked" them and handed out flowers to
be used as a means of "showing their colors." In a "War of
the Roses" reminiscent of the governor's campaign of 1886
between brothers Bob and Alf Taylor, the Antis adopted red
roses as their emblem, the Suffs yellow roses. Addressing
the legislators on the opening day of the session, Governor
Roberts urged ratification "in justice to the womanhood of
America."

A head count by suffrage leaders showed the Senate apparently safe, but a couple of test votes in the House had shown only fifty votes for the cause, the bare constitutional majority needed to win. Lawmakers, some from remote rural areas, found themselves the objects of attention by young ladies of both persuasions who wined and dined them in a manner that would match the tactics of some present-day lobbyists.

There were reports of bribes and the use of "ladies of the evening" as persuaders along with rumors of kidnappings. One legislator was assigned a bodyguard and Governor Roberts was threatened.

On Friday, August 13, the motion to ratify the suffrage amendment passed the Senate by a vote of twenty-five to four. The following Wednesday the measure came to a vote in the House. The Suffragists had thought their winning vote would come from twenty-four-year-old Harry T. Burn of Athens, but Burn showed up wearing a red rose. The Speaker of the House called for a vote on the motion to concur with the Senate resolution. To the surprise of nearly everyone, Burn, when his name was called, quickly responded with an "aye."

That one vote turned out to be the one that was needed. Pandemonium broke out. Tennessee had become the thirty-sixth state to ratify the nineteenth amendment. Harry Burn was the man of the hour. But what changed his mind?

The next day he took the floor to tell how it happened. On the morning of the vote, he had received a letter from his mother, Mrs. J. L. Burn of Niota. It read:

Dear Son:

> Hurrah, and vote for suffrage! Don't keep them in doubt. I notice some of the speeches against. They were bitter. I have been watching to see how you stood, but have not noticed anything yet. Don't forget to be a good boy and help Mrs. Catt put the "rat" in ratification.
>
>   Your Mother

Burns told his colleagues, "I know that a mother's advice is always safest for her boy to follow, and my mother wanted me to vote for ratification."

The Illegitimate Child Who Became Governor

Thanks to Charles G. Neese, United States Senior Judge, Nashville

When Bennie Walter Wade was born in Newport in 1870, the odds that he would someday become governor of Tennessee were slight indeed. Little Bennie was an illegitimate child and if he ever became involved in a hot political campaign, his enemies would be sure to bring out the fact that his parents had not been legally wed.

Nevertheless, Bennie's father, in successfully arguing with the young woman who was carrying his child that she should not have an abortion, made the comment that the baby might be a son and he might someday become Tennessee's chief executive.

Bennie's father was a physician in Newport, L. W. Hooper, and his mother was a young woman of Italian-Irish descent, Sarah Wade. When she was unable to prevail upon Dr. Hooper to either marry her or abort their child, she placed the baby in an orphanage. When young Bennie was nine years old, he was claimed by Dr. Hooper.

Given the educational advantages that a successful physician could provide, Ben did well in school and at a young age served two terms in the General Assembly.

In 1910, he entered the race for governor, promising to

throw out the "machine" of Governor Malcolm R. "Ham" Patterson. He made good on the promise, following his first two-year term with a second one. Sure enough, the question of his lineage was raised during the campaign. Not denying that the charge was true, he made this comment, as told in his autobiography, *The Unwanted Boy* (University of Tennessee Press, 1963): "The people of Tennessee are not so greatly concerned about where I came from as they are about where I am going and what I will do when I get there."

In addition to his service in the legislature and as governor, Hooper served briefly as a chancellor and, by presidential appointment, as a member and sometimes chairman (1922–25) of the United States Railroad Board.

In 1953, Tennessee held its first constitutional convention since 1870, the year Hooper was born. Among the distinguished people who made up that assembly was the eighty-three-year-old Ben W. Hooper. Much was made of the fact that he was the oldest delegate, a former governor, and one of a small number of Republicans. But the matter of who his parents were had long since been forgotten.

Governor Austin Peay, Man of Distinction

Thanks to Charles G. Neese, United States Senior Judge, Nashville

Nowadays an aspirant for statewide or regional elective office can, if he or she has the wherewithal, become known widely through television and other mass media. There was a time, however, when about the only way to gain name- and face-recognition was to manage a political campaign for another candidate. This prompted many persons to assume the duties of director of a campaign who otherwise would not have made themselves available.

One such person was Austin Peay, Esquire, a prominent and distinguished lawyer who was a native Kentuckian practicing in Clarksville. He dressed as if he had "just stepped out a bandbox," wearing high-tipped celluloid collars, carrying a gold-tipped walking cane, and sitting grandly alone in the back seat of his automobile as it was driven by a uniformed chauffeur.

Nobody complained about lawyer Peay's elegant appearance as he directed the campaign of Governor Malcolm Rice "Ham" Patterson, but when in 1922 he became a candidate for the Tennessee gubernatorial nomination himself, his manager and counsellors told him he needed to dress less formally and generally act more informal if he expected to establish rapport with the common folk out on the campaign trail.

"No," candidate Peay responded, "I shall continue to live as I always have lived. If the majority of Democrats don't want me as I am as their nominee, and if I am nominated, a majority of the voters of Tennessee don't want Austin Peay as he is and always has been, then I don't want to serve them as their governor."

He was nominated and elected governor of Tennessee in 1922 and renominated and reelected in 1924 and 1926. He went to his grave in September 1927 dressed in death as he always had been in life—to the nines.

Brains vs. Brawn

Thanks to Charles G. Neese, United States,
Senior Judge, Nashville

J.B. (Buck) Avery, Sr., of Alamo was a judge of the Tennessee Court of Appeals. Before that he was a member of the Tennessee Railroad and Public Utilities Commission, and before that he was Referee in Bankruptcy for the Western District of Tennessee. Preceding all those positions of honor was Judge Avery's run for the Democratic nomination for district attorney general.

Judge Avery was a huge man and his manner of movement created the impression that he was even bigger than he actually was. His chief opponent, from nearby Trenton, was Limmie Lee Harrell, small enough to be a jockey in horse races at county fairs in the area.

The candidates had a joint speaking during the campaign and, to indulge in a little levity, Avery commented that Harrell was "not big enough for the job."

"Why, if I wanted to," Avery continued, "I could just eat him up in one bite."

When it came time for Harrell to speak, he retorted to this jibe: "Well, Mr. Avery might be able to gobble me up in one bite; but, if he did, he'd have a helluva lot more brains in his stomach than he's got now in his big old head!"

Harrell won the nomination and the office!

Index

F 436.5 .I7 1986

It happened in Tennessee

GAYLORD MG